S0-CPE-434

ALSO  BY  GRANT  TREVITHICK


QUANTUM SPIRITUALITY:
A Journey of Personal Discovery

**QUANTUM POWER OF THOUGHT**
*(due late 2003)*

# 5 Secrets
## to
# Self-Love

by

Grant Trevithick

Quantum Spirituality Press ♦ New Jersey ♦ 2003

Quantum Spirituality Press
All Rights Reserved.
Copyright © 2003 by Grant Trevithick in the United States of America

Published by:
Quantum Spirituality Press
P. O. Box 529
Chester, New Jersey 07930-0088
Email: quantum.spirituality@erols.com
Phone: 908.876.3517

No part of this book may be reproduced or transmitted in any form or by any means, graphic, electronic, or mechanical, including photocopying, recording, taping, or by any information storage or retrieval system, without the permission in writing from the publisher. For additional information, please visit our website: www.self-love.com

**_Publisher's Cataloging-in-Publication Data_**
(Provided by Quality Books, Inc.)

Trevithick, Grant
    5 Secrets to Self-Love/ Grant Trevithick – 1st ed.
    iv, 151 p., 22.86 cm.
    Includes bibliographical references and index.
    LLCN: 2002093411
    ISBN: 1-58937-092-9 (Soft Cover)

    1. Spiritual life. 2. Life. I. Title

BF575.L8T74 2003                    158.1
                                     QB133-747

Printed in the United States of America

One dollar of the proceeds from each book sold will be donated to the Cheryl Wormser Trevithick Endowed Scholarship Fund, benefiting elementary education students at the University of Delaware. (Cheryl Wormser Trevithick Endowed Scholarship Fund, Office of University Development, University of Delaware, The Academy Building, Newark, DE 19716-0701)

*To Cheryl,*

*My best friend, my love, my inspiration, my wife:*
*Your courage stands as a monument to the human soul.*

# CONTENTS

From the teachings of *Patanjali*, we find Truth revealed:
*"As the removal of earth by a farmer digging a ditch*
*Opens up a channel for water to flow to his crops,*
*So the removal of obstacles by the student opens up*
*A channel for Cosmic Energy to flow into his being."*

# Introduction

Shame, desperation, and loneliness were emotions that filled my life. For almost 30 years, a deep, dark secret "dictated" my life. I labored heavily to keep this secret hidden from everyone in my life, even my closest personal friends and family. I could not bear the possibility that even one single person would learn this terrible secret. Surely, if anyone learned of my secret they could never love me. But everything I did seemed to advertise this secret, to highlight it to others.

The secret that kept me imprisoned in a life filled with pain and loneliness was . . . *I was unlovable.* I was living in my own personal hell. I was spending my entire life-energy hiding myself from all those around me, dreading that anyone might learn my secret. I kept myself hidden away, locked in a soul-dungeon with no chance of intimacy or peace of heart, all because I believed "I was unlovable" and many of my actions and behaviors provided validation of that belief.

Then I learned how to escape, to find a way out of this prison. I learned I was not alone in my incarceration; in truth, I shared this prison sentence with many millions of other people. I also saw that nearly everyone around me was imprisoned by the same beliefs.

I learned I had created this prison for myself; but I also found out that my imprisonment was not a life sentence: I was in a position to re-create a life that was very different from the one I had known. I found that I could transform my life of loneliness and pain into a life filled with love, peace of heart, and peace of mind. I learned the five simple "secrets" that were the keys to this prison. And I finally discovered that this time of imprisonment was an integral step on the path to enlightenment, a discovery that allowed me to be grateful for those painful experiences.

I wish the same blessing for you. Please accept this work as my personal gift, from one soul to another. No words I could ever write will offer you any form of "salvation" (whatever that term means to you). The ideas and concepts I will share with you do, however, offer what I hope will be an enlightening perspective on why we create lives that are the equivalent of "hell on earth." I will also offer five principles on how you can be free of this experience. I will share how to transform your current experiences into the realization of your own divinity.

I believe that this book will provide you with the answer to why we generate so much pain and suffering in our lives, and I believe it will share with you the keys that will transform this experience into one of love and joy. Throughout this book, you will learn you were, to begin with, engineered at the divine genetic level to generate an entire belief system based on a lack of Self-love. Then you will see how you—and countless other human beings—create an entire life's experience based on this very kind of belief system. You will also learn how this experience comes to serve you as you transform your life's experience from one of pain and suffering into one of love and joy. Finally, you will learn for yourself how this is your Divine Path—one absolutely necessary for you to reach self-enlightenment and the self-realization of your divinity.

Now, I'm not sitting here typing these words as if I were some wise sage or self-proclaimed, divinely inspired guru. I do not sit here claiming to have spent years earning a long list of initials after my name, signifying years upon years of theoretical academic research and schooling. I sit here typing these words, opening my heart and sharing my journey with you, as one person who has been schooled in the common, sometimes seemingly unhallowed, halls of life. I am nothing more than an ordinary man with more than forty years of living a human experience, the same as everyone else, the same as you.

During the majority of that time I was deathly afraid that someone might figure out that I was not a lovable human being. I spent my entire youth trying to fit in, trying to be cool (the word we used in my day); then I spent half of my adulthood working far harder than I ever had to in order to prove myself lovable. I spent an enormous amount of energy working to make myself look smart, trying to project an image of a lovable person to earn people's respect and love. Then I woke up when I was almost thirty years old, heartbroken to realize that, in spite of all that effort and in spite of all those fears, all that energy had been expended for naught. As hard as I worked, as hard as I tried, I was never able to earn anyone's love; instead, all I did was drive people away by my lack of genuineness.

My awakening began one morning, when I awoke and realized that every part of my life was filled with struggle and pain. I distinctly remember the words that echoed through my shattered heart: "There has to be more in life than this! Certainly no God would create us just to watch us suffer so much."

I don't know why some people begin to ask that eternal question— "Is there more to life than this?"—earlier than others do, while some people never seem to ask the question. All I know is that everyone on this planet experiences the same process; we all walk down the same path. Some of us stop long enough in the midst of our suffering to ask, "Is there more to life than this?" And those who wonder about the greater purpose of life are the people who have begun the journey from denial and suffering to the journey of self-realization.

While this path is relatively *simple*, it certainly is not *easy*. However, it is a journey that I personally could not imagine not taking. It is a journey that has led me out of the bondage of my old beliefs and into the Promised Land. I presume that, since you are reading this book, you are on that same journey.

It has been twelve years now since I lay awake in bed that Saturday morning, took a long, hard look at my life, and saw nothing but failure and pain. At that moment I began to realize that, as smart as I thought I was,

I did not know how to live a life of love and joy. I'm not sure I would have even known what love and joy were if I had experienced them at that time. But after awakening from my denial and becoming conscious of my beliefs and behaviors, I began my own journey from suffering with a heart filled with insecurities to enjoying a heart filled with a gentle sense of my Self-worth.

No, my journey has not been easy. It's been filled with many bumps, littered with potholes, and strewn with many mistakes along the way. It took almost a decade of research and heartfelt self-analysis and retrospection before I began to see the dynamics behind my sense of not being lovable. Carl Jung was most definitely correct when he stated, "Analysis is like surgery without anesthesia." But once I had marched through the muck and mire of my soul, after finally realizing the purpose of this struggle in the Grand Design, I found the keys to overcoming my self-incarcerating beliefs.

For the past dozen years I have studied most of the great teachings on this planet, from Eastern philosophies to the Western religions. And, although some of the ancient teachings discuss the journey through the pain of a lack of Self-love to the goal of self-realization somewhat metaphorically, I failed to find in the major teachings any of the keys to obtaining Self-love. Nevertheless, I learned these keys to the prison of feeling unlovable and how to be released from this prison, and I wish to share them with you in this book.

I have heard more times than I can count (maybe you have, too), "You have to learn to love your Self before you can love someone else." Well, I believe that everyone's greatest desire is to love another person completely and to feel that love being returned. But because most of us experience the lack of Self-love, our greatest desires as humans are being frustrated. And no wonder: No matter how hard we try to make relationships work, on any level, *we can never realize their full potential until we make our relationship with ourselves work first.*

That hope is exactly what this book will offer you. I will share with you the simple, step-by-step principles you need to forge a new relationship with your Self. You will learn how to respect and honor your Self, and as you do you will experience a deepening, blossoming love of your Self. I am not talking about the kind of egoistic, maniacal pseudo-self-regard we often see around us. I'm speaking of a deep, profound sense that you are a lovable person, a knowing that you deserve to have the greatest gifts the Universe has to offer, and to experience enough love within yourself to share yourself deeply and intimately with the people in your lives. You will find peace in who you are; you will find peace in your heart; and you will finally come to realize that you are a lovable human being merely because you breathe. I invite you to allow me to share, as my personal gift to you, the lessons that have taken me painful years to learn. I would like to share these with you so that you can leap ahead on your own path and learn these lessons with the least amount of pain and suffering.

In truth, the single greatest problem facing mankind today is not starving children in Africa, the AIDS epidemic, poverty, racism, or any of the other issues that seem to become so prominent in the media during election years. Although these certainly are issues we ought to be concerned about, the single greatest issue facing mankind is nothing new or unique to this generation, or even to this millennium. This one issue is the root of all suffering, the root of all pain; this belief is the root of what many people refer to as "evil." This greatest of issues is a lack of Self-love.

If everyone felt secure in and of himself or herself, there would be no need for pride, ego, machismo, or to have to "prove oneself." If everyone felt a deep sense of Self-love, if everyone respected himself or herself and others, then no one would feel the need for angry, violent exchanges. If everyone really felt a deep sense of gentle Self-love and respect, we all would have enough love in our hearts to share with those less fortunate. There would be no famine, there would be no crime, no racism, no poverty—in short, nothing for the politicians to campaign on—and that just might be the greatest definition of Nirvana I've heard so far.

So we are going to explore the origins of this belief that we are "not lovable," the spiritual and genetic engineering that causes each of us to experience these feelings, and the impact this belief has on our lives. Our journey will continue through a very different understanding of our divine purpose on this planet, which will be followed by a detailed discussion of the three phases of our path here, the path we call life. Building upon this foundation, we will continue on to delve into the Five Secrets to Self-Love. We will investigate each secret in depth and walk away with simple, easy-to-understand, step-by-step techniques to implement them into our lives.

After years of detailed investigation and research into the Eastern philosophies (i.e., Taoism, Zen Buddhism, Sufism, Sikhism, Hinduism), the Western religions (i.e., the mystical aspects of Judaism from the *Kabbalah*, what Jesus taught us from both the New Testament and the extra-canonical Gospels), and modern science (i.e., quantum mechanics, relativity physics, modern medicine, psychology), I have come to realize that all these teachings and disciplines in fact teach one set of Truths. From this foundation I will share the following material with you. Again, please accept this book as my gift, from one soul to another.

# Part One:

# A New Perspective

It is all a process of change, of transformation, of refining transparency. There is no light without darkness. Many feel that darkness denotes something negative, but in the nighttime, the stars twinkle and in the nighttime the dreams grow, and those dreams determine our tomorrow. So nighttime, daytime, they are parts of the dream. One is neither bad nor good. It is how we approach those times that determines their value in our own life. So let us not fear the dark.[1]

— Ywahoo Dhyani, Cherokee medicine man

$M$an makes his life so complex; he brings upon himself
an avalanche of confusion, pain and suffering; he is driven by
desires of the mind and of the body, both enslaving him.
Yet the way to freedom is simple, so simple that most pass it
by. Learn to listen to the voice of the Master.[1]

– White Eagle

## Chapter One

# You Are Not Alone

**Please don't believe a single word you read in this book. Please don't accept a single idea or perspective you read in this book.** That is, unless, as you read this book, you have deep-seated feelings that these words and these ideas *are* the Truth. Don't accept anything you read here unless you can see how applying these ideas and principles to your life will bring you closer to living the life you really wish you were living today.

I certainly had heard "God is love" before. I was surprised to realize that Truth and love were maybe the same thing. Was Truth also a vibrational pattern? The words "ring of truth" ran through my head. Truth is a felt vibrational pattern. When something is true it "rings" true. When a horseshoe fitter tests a horseshoe, he strikes it to hear the ring. Bad metal rings falsely.[2]

— Fred Alan Wolf, Ph.D.

If you read something in this book that does not make sense, I invite you to resist dismissing the entire work outright; rather, I invite you to place that one concept or idea aside and continue reading. If you feel the need to take my ideas and concepts and tailor them to your individual perspective of life, then please feel free to do so. I offer this book to you for your consideration only, in hope that you may find this material contributes to your beginning to live the life your heart most desires to experience.

## You are not alone

*The world is filled with wonderful people, and I'm the only one who is not lovable, not worthy*—or so I thought. I felt that I was not lovable, that I was not

3

worthy, that I was not a good person. If these feelings were not painful enough, I felt ashamed of having these feelings. I also felt I was alone in having these feelings, which only made me feel even more unlovable.

I saw people every day doing wonderful things, getting credit they sometimes deserved, and many times getting credit or acknowledgment they did not deserve. Whenever I decided I wanted to get some credit and acknowledgment, I

> The soul attracts that which it secretly harbors; that which it loves, and also that which it fears; it reaches the height of its cherished aspirations; it falls to the level of its unchastened desires; and circumstances are the means by which the soul receives its own.[3]
>
> — James Allen

tried to put myself in the position to receive acknowledgment. I worked very hard putting forth the maximum effort, and yet nothing I ever did seemed to generate that feeling that I was lovable. It always seemed to backfire, and I only received negative feedback instead. For me, this was just further validation that I was unlovable and would never be able to earn respect and love.

Virtually every person on this planet is addicted to "being right," and I certainly was no exception. I lived with the strong belief that I was unlovable; as my life unfolded, I experienced life's normal events just as everyone else does. But I interpreted these events and circumstances through the filter of my belief that "I'm not lovable." Of course, I then interpreted virtually all the events and circum-

> The mind is an organ system that includes all of the physical being. The purpose of the mind is to survive and be right. To these ends it will do anything.[4]
>
> — Ron Smothermon, M.D.

stances of my life as further evidence that my original belief was correct. So my foundational belief—that I was unlovable—seemed validated time and time again.

Now, each time this occurred, I got to be "right" one more time. Even when my circumstances provided me evidence that I *was* lovable, I didn't see this evidence because it would not allow me to "be right"—according to my skewed beliefs. Just like everyone else, I love to be right, and in order to do so I interpreted my experiences in such a way that I continually validated my beliefs. This left me feeling good about being "right," yet it also perpetuated my feelings of being unlovable.

Because I believed deep down inside that I was unlovable, not worthy, I interpreted anything and everything through the filter of "I'm unlovable." When I heard or read anything that might possibly be interpreted as critical or judgmental towards me, my mind interpreted this as further evidence that I was indeed unlovable. When I was in the midst of feeling unlovable, I only heard and saw the world through a blizzard of harsh and critical comments. Everything I saw, everything I heard, everything seemed to be validating my worst fear—that I was unlovable. Someone could say ten really nice things about me and only slightly mention one comment that might have the smallest hint of something that might possibly sound like criticism. In this case, I'd only hear the criticism, and I'd hear it as the harshest of criticism.

Whenever I sensed the slightest possibility that something good might come into my life, I used to sabotage it because I did not feel worthy of receiving the good. When someone attempted to give me a great gift, I would not accept it because, once again, I did not feel worthy to receive the good. I might even work hard towards a particular goal, but once I was in sight of achieving this goal, I procrastinated or just didn't finish the last few small steps towards accomplishing my goal. Then when the opportunity I had sought ceased to present itself, this served as still one more bit of validation that I was not lovable, that I was not worthy of receiving the good that life that can offer.

One of my lifelong habits was to deflect any compliment paid to me with a self-deprecating humor. If someone told me that he thought I was very intelligent, then I replied with something like, "Well, I've been reading since I was only eighteen." Or I would explain that the reason he thought that I was intelligent was not really what it seemed.

For example, I remember one time when I was talking to a friend about one of my passions, a subject (Eastern philosophies) which I actually know quite a bit about. My friend observed that I sounded pretty smart and knowledgeable. I actually felt somewhat embarrassed and quickly replied that I had just seen a documentary on the Discovery Channel about the history of Buddhism. What I was really telling my friend was that I did not deserve to be thought of highly, that I wasn't smart enough to receive the compliment. You see, that's exactly what I was telling my Self with my behavior. So while I worked very hard to make people think I was smart, once they did I immediately invalidated their compliment. Now this behavior seems rather bizarre to me. I expended a great deal of energy to earn someone's respect, and then when I finally had it, I denied it both to myself and to that person. And it's in just this way that lack of Self-love shows up in many of our lives.

While I have just described behaviors and thoughts that dominated my life for more than thirty years, I no longer believe I was alone in these. I have read numerous books and articles and talked to thousands of people, and I have come to the conclusion that these sorts of beliefs and behaviors are fairly universal. So if you have felt these feelings, if you hold the same beliefs about yourself that I did about me, be assured you are not alone. These beliefs are universal—and they're also self-perpetuating.

In many different ways, the feelings and beliefs that we are unlovable manifest themselves throughout our lives, making it difficult for others to love us. All these feelings and behaviors only validate our worst inner fear: that we are indeed unlovable. Furthermore, along with these feelings we hold the belief that somehow we have been singled out, that each of us is the only person having these feelings.

This belief only magnifies our feelings of shame and seems to further validate our beliefs that we are unlovable. Feeling alone and ashamed, we often put forth great efforts to make sure nobody around us becomes aware of our terrible secret. We overcompensate for our perceived short-comings. We try to make intelligent comments if we're afraid we are unlovable because we are not smart enough. We spend hours on our make-up and looks if we're afraid we are unlovable because we are not good-looking enough. Or we go out of our way to serve other people if we believe we are not lovable just because of who we are.

When we try to be something more or different than we naturally are in order to prove or to win respect and love, the impression we give our audience is of someone who is trying to be something he or she is not by nature. Our audience almost immediately picks up on this behavior and can quickly see how we feel about ourselves. So, our worst fears come true because of our very efforts. While we work hard to hide our terrible secret, we're the ones making sure everyone around knows exactly how we feel about ourselves. It seems like a no-win, catch-22 situation. The harder we work, the worse things get. And every person on the planet experiences this cycle to some degree.

## Every single person on this planet experiences issues with Self-love. You are not alone.

These issues contribute to our lives in varying degrees. For some of us, these issues dominate every waking moment of our lives and probably even into our sleep. Those of us so afflicted live every moment in a desperate panicky state, spending all our lives running from these feelings. We spend all our life energies attempting to hide and overcompensate for a lack of Self-love (sometimes these feelings even show up as self-*loathing*). For others of us, these feelings may only occasionally show up as blips on the radar screen while we're searching for our happiness; lack of Self-love does not cause much pain and suffering for such folks.

Each of us, so it seems, has had something happen to us during our early childhood days that seems to trigger these feelings of lack of Self-esteem or Self-love. We seem to be going along fine during our young days on this planet, and then an event occurs that alters our perspective. This event becomes a defining moment in our lives. It is from this event or events that we create our belief that we are not lovable. This belief then permeates our entire identity, creating a deep-seated base of fear from which many of us develop our entire sense of Self.

Please allow me to share the example of this event in my own life. Perhaps reading my story will allow you to relate to this dynamic in your own history.

I distinctly remember this event, even though I was only around four years old when it occurred. I took a toy from my older brother, who then complained to my father. Sensing that this was a great opportunity to teach me that taking what wasn't mine was inappropriate behavior, my father sent me to my room. He then told me to stay there until he called and let me out. He told me that this would allow me to get a taste of being in jail, which is "where you're headed if you don't learn that taking other people's possessions is wrong."

Up to now, everything was just fine. There in my room I interpreted this event as that I was properly being punished for something that I did wrong. But as the day wore on and I played with all the different toys in my room, I began to get bored. Time began to slow down and I began to get frustrated. Finally, dinnertime came along, and my mother called for all us children to come to the dining room to eat (this was back in the days when families still ate together in the evenings).

I did not come when called as usual, so my mother came looking for me and found me in my room. She asked me why I didn't come when she called, and I told her that Dad sent me to my room and said I could not come out until he told me to. (In those days, fathers tended to set the rules of the household and act as the primary disciplinarians.)

Soon thereafter, my father came to my room and asked me why I was still there when my mother had called everyone for dinner. I reminded him of his instructions earlier that day. He then told me that he had forgotten I was in my room, and that I had "been dumb" to have stayed in there that long. He also said, "You should have reminded me earlier. I didn't mean for you to spend the entire day there."

Now, what did my four-year-old mind hear in what my father said? "I forgot about you, you are not important enough for me to remember you—and you weren't even smart enough to remind me. So you're not worthy of my love." Just to be clear on this point, this was not what my father actually said; this is only what *I heard him say inside my brain*, as the interpretation of a four-year-old mind.

Yet I walked away from that simple event hearing my father, the person I admired and respected most, telling me I was not smart enough to be loved. I was devastated at this new revelation: *I wasn't smart enough to be lovable.* What a terrible realization! Certainly, I thought, I must keep this horrible truth to myself; I must not let anyone know. If anyone else ever finds out the truth about me, they won't love me, either.

*How flawed I must be,* I thought inside me, *that my own father has told me that I was not lovable.* I felt ashamed and completely alone. And although I never went through a conscious thought process, I decided within myself then and there that I was going to have to create a new identity that could hide this terrible secret. With this new identity I would prove to everyone that I was smart enough to be loved, that I was a lovable person.

All this happened in a mere instant, and in that instant I began to define the persona called "Grant." Before this situation happened, I was just being Grant. Now, since I'd learned that just being Grant wasn't being a lovable person, I began to define a new identity called "Grant." I created an identity that I hoped might be lovable, because I believed the person I was inside was not lovable. But I really built this identity to hide the real Grant and to project a false persona, one built from a foundation of fear.

I began to work to prove my intelligence to everyone around me on a constant basis. Whenever I thought of an intelligent statement to make, regardless of whether or not it was appropriate to the audience or the conversation at the time, I made sure to interject it into the conversation. I had to; I had to show people that I was smart enough to be loved.

> The lower self is obsessed with presenting itself in ways that gain the good opinion of others. This results in increase of possessions and pride in them, as well as arrogance, self-importance, and contempt.[5]
>
> — Sufi Sheikh Kashani

After a while I grew desperate in my attempts to prove how smart, how lovable I was. I began to tell lies about accomplishments I never achieved, trying to persuade my audience I was intelligent, I was good enough, I was lovable. Every time I did this, I was telling my Self that I was not lovable just because of who I was. I was telling my Self that I was only lovable if my audience believed all these invented stories. Even when I did accomplish something wonderful, I felt the need to exaggerate the feat and then to brag about it. I was really telling my Self that the only reason someone would love me was because of what I had accomplished, not because of who I was. I developed a complete identity, a complete persona, all to prove I was smart enough to be loved, that I was worthy of being loved. I did all this because I was deathly afraid someone might learn the terrible truth about me, how unlovable and how dumb I really was.

Even when people did tell me they loved me, I couldn't believe them. I felt they only loved this persona I had created. I thought, *If they only knew the truth about me, they would never love me.* So I created this catch-22 situation: I wanted to be loved in the worst way; I was desperate to have people love me; and yet I created a situation in which I would never feel loved. Even when people told me they loved me in spite of myself, I could not believe them. They could only be in love with this false identity I had created. Talk about a no-win situation!

One of the strangest ironies on this planet is this: When a person exerts effort to prove to those around him that he is smart, the only impression he leaves is of someone who is trying to prove that he is smart. Generally people can sense when someone else is making a concerted effort to create an impression, and they walk away sensing that the person is not being genuine or honest. **Every time someone works to create the impression of being smart, or lovable, or any other impression, the effort always backfires to leave the audience with just the opposite impression.** How many times have you heard someone tell you how smart he is, and the thought that runs through your mind is, "If he's really smart, he wouldn't have to tell everyone."

While I was watching *Oprah* recently with my wife, I heard another person's "defining" story. Oprah Winfrey was talking about how certain events occur in childhood and define our entire lives, and one member of the audience named Carmen shared her story. When she was about six years old, Carmen was an intelligent, confident, and self-assured child. One day in school, Carmen was asked to go to the front of her classroom and perform a math problem on the blackboard. Just as she got to the front of the

> Ernest Hemingway wrote, "The world breaks everyone, and after, many are strong at the broken places." This truth is difficult for most of us to accept. We focus on the brokenness and never take notice that we have become stronger at the broken places. Yes! When fractures heal, they become stronger than the bone.[6]
>
> — Bernie Siegel, M.D.

class, she got nervous and her mind went completely blank. Psychologists would refer to this as performance anxiety. She just stood in front of the blackboard, embarrassed that she didn't know how to work the problem on the blackboard. She stood there staring at the board, while her teacher quickly became frustrated with her.

Rather than have Carmen sit back down, her teacher made her stand there in front of the class for an extended (for a child) period of time, most likely five to ten minutes. Short as that period was, it seemed like a lifetime to this little girl. She felt humiliated, stupid, and ashamed. Carmen just stood in front of the class, her mind completely blank, her nervousness building. Her mind began to race, "What are all my classmates thinking of me? What is the teacher thinking of me? This is a simple problem—why don't I know the answer? Everyone must think I am pretty stupid." Her mind filled with embarrassment, shame, and her mind generated the interpretation that she must not be lovable because she was so dumb.

9

FIVE SECRETS TO SELF-LOVE

Can you see it? In less than an instant, this once confident, vivacious young girl decided that she was "dumb" and was unlovable. From those five minutes on, she spent the rest of her life believing she wasn't smart, believing she wasn't lovable, afraid that anyone else on this planet would learn the horrible truth about her. She became so increasingly shy, she could barely speak to anyone, even her family. Eventually she came to avoid all risk in her life; she barely left her house other than to maintain a meager existence at work. She suffered a lifetime without people, a lifetime without intimacy, a lifetime of missed opportunities, a lifetime wasted—and it all emanated from five minutes of nervousness.

I heard another such story recently, about a man named Billy. As a young boy Billy was experimenting, exploring the world he lived in. One of the wonders he was learning about was a book of matches. He saw his parents smoke every day, and he stared astonished every time he saw fire created from a seemingly simple piece of paper.

Billy recalled the day he was sitting behind the garage, striking matches against the book, just as his parents did every day. But as soon as he managed to get one lit, the flame scared him and he dropped the match—right onto a pile of dried leaves. They quickly caught on fire and sent flames against the wood garage, which was soon engulfed in flames. The fire trucks came and the local firefighters saved most of Billy's home. After a quick investigation, the firefighters blamed the fire on some faulty wiring, which was next to some old cans of paint thinner in the garage.

No one asked Billy if he knew what had caused the fire, but from then on he felt guilty for never telling his parents. In fact, he carried his guilt around with him every day of his life. Billy felt that he was a terrible person for having done this to his family, and then he felt even more worthless because, although he didn't lie to them, he also had never told them the truth. Billy lived his entire life from childhood believing he was a terrible person based on this one experience.

To compensate for these feelings, Billy became what is often referred to as a "drama king" (they call women who exhibit this behavior "drama queens"). Everything Billy did turned dramatic, with him saving the day. Billy exaggerated things that happened in his daily life. With him, a minor scrape became a life-threatening wound. With his theatrics he kept everyone away from the person inside. The only person he allowed anyone to interact with was the actor that Billy continually portrayed. And Billy was terrified that someone would find out about him, and he, too, couldn't bear the shame of anyone knowing how unlovable he "really" was.

Then there was Francesca, an adventurous young girl whose parents considered her a tomboy. Her mother, raised in the old school, was concerned because Francesca always liked wearing pants and exploring the world with her older brothers rather than staying at home and playing with dolls. As much as her mother tried to entice Francesca to become a "normal girl," she was only interested in playing sports with the boys. Her brothers and several of her friends observed this behavior and occasionally teased Francesca about being a tomboy instead of a "normal" girl.

One day, several of Francesca's older brother's friends made fun of her; they kept telling her she was really a boy trapped in a girl's body. They began to yell names at her. Her brother's friends told her that her parents really wanted a girl so they were dressing her up in girl's clothes even though underneath it all she was a little boy. Young children can be so cruel at times, without ever really understanding the pain they inflict. In an instant Francesca suddenly started to believe their youthful teasing. She began to cry and rode her bicycle home in tears. From that moment on, Francesca forced herself to become the typical example of what was expected of every young girl in those days. She began to play with dolls. She began to dress in frilly dresses. She did all these things, not because doing so made her happy, but rather because she felt she wouldn't be lovable if she really followed her heart.

Francesca married young, had several children, and created a typical home for her family. But while she was doing all this, she was miserable inside because she knew this was not who she really was. Francesca was convinced that if she ever showed her more adventurous, daring, energetic side everyone would know she was not lovable.

Let me share one final story with you to illustrate this point. A good friend of mine named Wanda was born physically challenged, with several genetic physical birth defects. She was born without the use of her legs, which were malformed and nonfunctional. As a very young child, Wanda was bright and always quick to smile. The first years of her life were filled with laughter and giggling. Her joy was infectious, and if you saw Wanda, her parents told me, you had to smile in reply to her constant grin. Wanda loved life and seemed to always enjoy herself.

But then as she grew older, things changed. Wanda watched her siblings run, jump, and do all the things "normal" children did. Her physical challenges kept her from participating with the other neighborhood children, and, watching from her wheelchair at the window of her home, she always felt left out, "less-than." For hours while her parents thought she was in her room reading or doing her homework, Wanda would sit in front of the window in her bedroom watching the other children play outside. These children did not understand Wanda's condition and avoided her. She felt all alone, rejected, and ashamed. The more she watched them play, the more they ran and laughed and had a great time, the more Wanda felt like she must be "less-than" because of her physical limitations.

At some point in her early childhood, Wanda decided that she wasn't lovable because of her physical impairments. After this decision, she grew distant from people and began to build a "poor me" consciousness. She constantly complained about her lot in life; she let everyone around know how challenged she felt and how unfair her life was. Eventually her behavior and her constant, never-ending barrage of complaints and negativity drove away even those who loved her. She never let anyone close to her because she felt so unlovable.

Wanda, Francesca, Billy, and Carmen are not alone. After reading hundreds of books and talking to literally thousands of people over the last decade, I have come to the conclusion that every single person on this planet undergoes similar experiences and interpretations from their early years. From these experiences and their related interpretations, **every person on the planet has developed a certain level of fear-based belief, the feeling of being unlovable.** Some of these beliefs are so great they dominate virtually every aspect of the person's life. Others are less so, and only show up occasionally. This feeling of being unlovable is universal; everyone experiences it to some degree or another.

Now, I don't want to dwell too much on the negativity this belief causes you, because that only makes you feel even worse about your Self. That certainly should not be the goal of any material offering to help people transform these beliefs into positive, constructive Self-images. Instead, it is important for you to be aware that having these feelings is completely normal.

Everyone, present and past, has had the opportunity to experience these same feelings to one degree or another. Everyone who has yet to be born is also destined to have these beliefs and feelings. *You are not alone in your feelings.* In fact, **you have no choice but to have these feelings; you were genetically designed at the DNA level, you were created at the spiritual level to not only experience these feelings but to create a life based on these feelings. This is part of the Divine Plan, or the Grand Design.**

# Spiritual Truths Discussed in this Chapter

**Every single person on this planet experiences issues with Self-love. You are not alone.**

Although you often feel alone when you feel a lack of Self-love, you are not alone. Every person on this planet either has had or will have the experience of a lack of Self-love. You are not alone. This is a normal part of the process called life.

**H**ow we feel about ourselves, the joy we get from living, ultimately depend directly on how the mind filters and interprets everyday experiences. Where we are happy depends on inner harmony, not on the controls we are able to exert over the great forces of the universe.[1]

— Mihaly Csikszentmihalyi, Ph.D.

## Chapter Two

# The Path to Enlightenment

I've often heard people suggest that the entire Universe, this planet, and all of its inhabitants, are the product of mere random chance. I've heard the proposition that with our entire scientific prowess and the latest technology we can't find definitive evidence of a Higher Power and therefore this Higher Power does not exist.

Well, not only do I disagree, but more and more of the scientific community disagrees, too. Many of our top scientists are coming to the conclusion that the only answer to their

> God spoke the world into being, the divine language is energy; the alphabet, elementary particles; God's grammar, the laws of nature. Many scientists have sensed a spiritual dimension in the search for these laws. For Einstein, discerning the laws of nature was a way to discover how God thinks.[2]
>
> — Daniel C. Matt, Ph.D.

findings is this: **God does exist. Not only does God exist, but the Universe operates based on a set of principles and within the framework of a Grand Design.** We shall see this Grand Design, or the Divine Path, revealed as we search for our answers to Self-love in this material.

Many of the most prominent scientific minds of the last century have come to the realization of God's presence. They have also gone so far as to suggest that God created this world using the scientific laws that we can now study. I believe the most extensive research will demonstrate just that—God did create this entire Universe using a set of Laws or principles. The Universe today operates on the very same set of principles. It is these principles that scientists are now studying in their efforts to understand *How the Universe Operates*. Spiritual teachers study the same Universe and attempt to answer the question, *Why was the Universe Created and why does it operate based on these principles?*

The answer lies within the realm of both disciplines: in order to fully understand the scientific realm you must answer the spiritual teachers' question, and vice versa. And understanding and overcoming feelings and beliefs that form a lack of Self-love requires this depth of perspective and understanding.

An old proverb tells of six blind men who attempt to describe an elephant. One man holds onto a leg and asserts that the elephant is like a tree trunk, round and solid. Another one holds onto the tail and says the elephant is like a whip, thin and flexible. The third man holds onto the trunk and describes the elephant as a hollow, flexible tube. And so on. While each is "right" from his limited perspective, it is only by viewing the elephant from a broader perspective that we can understand the nature of the *entire* elephant. So, like the proverbial six blind men, we also must expand our perspective to see the Grand Design. Or, to use another metaphor, it's all too easy to live our lives from our perspective only, never seeing the forest for the trees. We must step back out of the trees to see the beauty of the Grand Design that's inherent in the forest.

I can't imagine for a second that anyone who has stood on the precipice of the Grand Canyon and watched a sunset sink into the desert could imagine that this breathtaking scene was not designed by the divine imagination of a Higher Power. I can't imagine that the sunrise off the snow-capped mountains of the Rockies or the Alps can be anything less than the result of divine inspiration. For anyone who has witnessed the transformation of a caterpillar into the delicate beauty of the monarch butterfly, for anyone who has felt the power and sensuousness of a raging waterfall, for anyone who has experienced the unconditional love of the family pet, for anyone who has felt the energy gently flowing through our old growth forests—it's hard to consider that no Higher Power had a hand in this creation. I can't imagine that anyone who has heard the gentle giggle or laughter of a child at play could effectively argue that divinity does not pulse through this planet and all its inhabitants.

When we accept the premise of a Higher Power, for even a moment, then we must believe either that there is a Grand Design for humankind or that we are living our lives for the sheer amusement of this Higher Power, like the cosmic version of a circus. When I stop and look at my life, I'm sure I have provided many amusing moments to this Supreme Power, but I doubt that all we see around us is merely a form of a cosmic circus built for God's personal, morbid amusement.

Instead, when we take a few steps back and look at the entire "elephant," we instantly become aware of certain patterns in our lives. These patterns often become blurred in our day-to-day struggles to meet our monthly bills or maintain our personal relationships. We begin to see evidence of common experiences, and we begin to see common phases of life. We then become aware that **there exists a certain thematic consistency throughout all our lives. When we see that everyone on the planet experiences these same phases of life, we can only conclude that these phases must be part of the Grand Design. We begin to understand that we are genetically engineered at the DNA level to experience life in a certain manner.**

> What really interests me is whether God could have made the world differently; in other words, whether the demand for logical simplicity leaves any freedom at all.[3]
>
> — Albert Einstein

Because of this genetic programming, everyone on the planet experiences the same basic patterns during their lifetimes. While we do seem to be able to choose the pace of our individual paths, we all must experience the same basic path. The similarities in our paths offer the evidence to support one aspect of our Grand Design. The first stepping stone on this Path begins when we are children, full of exuberance and still deep in awe and wonder with all the miracles occurring in our new world.

Upon entering this world as wonder-filled children, we begin to learn how to survive in this world filled with dangers and traps. To help us do this, our parents naturally use fear to motivate us to avoid putting ourselves in dangerous positions. We begin to learn to become afraid of different parts of our environment, and we adopt fear-based beliefs about ourselves, accepting the belief that we are not lovable. We proceed on the divine path to generate lives that comprise pain and suffering, as is the natural result of fear-based beliefs. Many of us develop lives filled with pain and suffering and grief.

Yet this fear and the resulting pain serve a Higher Purpose. Because we now have a full experience of fear and pain, we can gain a deep understanding of the experience of love. It is through the contrasting experiences that man fully experiences the joy and bliss of living a life filled with love, which is our divine purpose, our divine destiny.

And once we understand the pathway towards Enlightenment, we can begin rebuilding our lives, transforming them from the pain of fear into the joy and bliss of love. Once we understand the path, we can accelerate our journey towards living lives filled with the abundance, prosperity, vitality, health, and pure joy that results from living from love.

And this path towards Enlightenment begins as a little child . . .

## As a child . . .

Everyone on this planet was born (or at least that's what I believe). I've talked to a few people in my life who claim to be products of some other union other than a man and a woman (some have even claimed to be from other planets or galaxies), but I have listened to them with more than a grain of salt (perhaps an entire truckload). We all enter this life on this planet as children, and as children we all shared the same characteristics: We were all full of joy and anticipation of the many possibilities that lay ahead of us in this adventure we call life. We were all as children filled with enthusiasm, and we were wonder-full expressions of our being.

Upon a child's introduction into this world, generally with lungs screaming from being taken from a nice cozy warm womb into the cold, sterile hospital maternity ward, his life is full of a love for exploration and of unfettered expressions of love for life. Almost from a child's first moment, he begins to exude wondrous love and begins freely expressing himself (or herself [1]). **From the first moment the child begins to smile, the first moment the child begins to express his personality, that child lives as a being of complete love. The young child does not know to be afraid.** He views life through a filter of faith that life is fun, a safe place in which to play and explore. The new child has not yet learned any fears; he is an unrestrained expression of joy and playfulness.

Young children are wonderful beings, absolute expressions of love and joy. Young children are unrelenting expressions of their being. They laugh, they giggle uncontrollably, they smile, they express joy and happiness, and they express all their emotions without a filter. Whatever they feel, they express. When a young child feels like laughing and giggling, bubbling over with joy and happiness, he or she does. A young child does not know or worry about any social taboos; a young child does not worry about the "have to's" or the "shoulds" or the "should nots." Sometimes children laugh, giggle, and express their joy so much that they annoy the adults who have learned that "respectable people" don't act "that way."

About fifteen years ago the Universe provided me with an example of this lesson. I was married in my late twenties to a wonderful lady, who by a previous marriage had a beautiful young daughter named Kendall. For the six years we were together, Kendall and I thoroughly enjoyed our relationship. One particular Easter stands out in my mind and served as an awesome reminder of the joy of childhood.

My wife and I completely decorated the house for the traditional Easter celebration. We hid several dozen eggs throughout the house, and we put a large stuffed Easter Bunny on the coffee table in the den. We set all this up so that Kendall would be sure to see it when she came downstairs for her Sunday cartoons. Sitting beside the stuffed bunny sat a basket filled with that annoying plastic grass and several mouth-watering, delicious

---

[1] I will use the term "him" or other derivatives of the masculine impersonal pronoun purely for the sake of expediency. I certainly don't mean that only males have these experiences or that there exists a separate Path depending on the sex of a person. Rather I refuse to stop the story repeatedly to ensure I refer to both sexes equally. Please forgive my laziness.

chocolate eggs. The setting was perfect, and we went to bed that night filled with eager anticipation of Kendall's reaction.

In the early morning, a scream that shook the rafters sat me up with a jolt. Thinking only the worst, I threw on a pair of jeans and rushed downstairs to find out what was wrong. I turned the corner—and saw this beautiful young girl about three-and-a-half years old. She flashed a grin that filled the entire room as she stared at the stuffed Easter Bunny and basket filled with chocolate treasures.

No description on earth can do justice to explaining the joy and love that shone through that young girl's face. As soon as my wife came downstairs, Kendall began her mission: finding each and every egg the Easter Bunny had left behind. Each time she found an egg, Kendall's face lit up with joy and she let out a gleeful scream. Within a few minutes she found almost all the eggs we'd hidden; so I sneakily grabbed a few from her basket and hid them again. I kept this up for at least a half an hour, during which time our house was never filled with so much love and joy. As she discovered each egg, Kendall let out another joyful scream, and each smile and gleeful scream let the world know exactly how she felt.

Now, I'm not sharing this story to burst anyone's bubble about the Easter Bunny (no, sorry, but there really isn't an Easter Bunny). I tell you this story only to remind you of the simple joy and pleasure you received from the simplest things in life when you were very young. Did you ever stare for hours in total wonder at those ants building their home? Didn't you find the greatest joy, just sitting in your grandfather's lap, swinging on the front porch, or watching the squirrels play in the front yard? Yes, all those Kodak and Lifesaver moments like these brought joy to each and every one of us. We didn't need new Ferraris to make us happy. It took only a simple gesture from another person or the beauty of nature to remind us that enough love exists in the Universe to fill all our hearts with joy. As we age, we often reflect back at these moments with a joyous remembrance.

## As children, we're unlimited expressions of love.

Young children see the world freshly and with newness each moment of the day. Everything they see is brand new to them, and so everything they see is miraculous. As adults, we have seen the same things every day, so we've become numb to it all. We hardly, if at all, even notice the miracles of life. We run through our daily routines and only very rarely stop long enough to notice the beauty of a sunset, the blossoming of the roses in the spring, or the miracle of life surrounding us at every turn. Children are not afflicted with this malady; they see everything as a miracle. Each day is a day of miraculous discovery.

This beautiful young girl named Kendall showed me yet another great lesson. We used to love to play together every day. One of our rituals was to take long walks in the park with Keisha, our half-collie, half-Siberian husky. One day when Kendall was around five years old, we were walking along the creek in the park across the road with Keisha. Kendall stopped to examine the ruin of a large tree, which high winds had pushed over the night before.

> Do not ask a child to tell You what is a miracle He may turn and ask you what In all the world you think is not.[4]
>
> — James Dillet Freement

Kendall looked at the inside of the tree, where wood ants had carved their home and seriously weakened the tree before it collapsed. Kendall asked me, "What are those lines and tunnels?" and I told her all about wood ants.

About two days later, Kendall and I were taking another walk along the same creek. This time one of Kendall's friends came along. Kendall beamed with pride as she showed her friend the tree and told her about the wood ants. I remember standing back with pride, watching this beautiful young lady explore the world and witnessing the discovery of one of the miracles of nature we take for granted each day.

It's the gift of a child—the absolute, unfiltered expression of joy and happiness, and the awe and wonder of the simplest miracles of life. During this first, childhood phase of life, we are unfettered expressions of our beings, without filters, without fears and inhibitions. When was the last time you saw an adult have a giggling fit? When a child wants to be hugged, he just naturally runs into a loved one's arms. Young children have not learned to be "socially acceptable," they have not learned to filter themselves according to what others might think. Young children simply are natural expressions of their beings; they have not yet learned to create images and false identities to hide behind.

When a child experiences anything new, he is naturally in awe and wonder. Children see miracles around them every day, in the simplest acts of nature. Young children see and experience the world as one miracle after another, one huge planet to explore and learn all about. Their youthful innocence exudes from every action and every thought.

Then the next stepping-stone on our Path to Enlightenment arrives, as we begin to learn about the concept of *duality*.

## The next step . . .

As young children, we don't even consider any other possibility than that the world is a loving, safe place for us to explore, to try new things out, and generally to play as much as we can. We crawl on the floor, we touch everything, we taste everything, we smile and laugh at almost everything, and we are absolute expressions of our Selves, without filters or worries.

Then our parents begin "parenting"—begin teaching us how to be safe in this new world. We learn that sticking anything metal into the electrical plug in the wall will cause us to be electrocuted, and we'll die. We learn that pulling down on the handle of a pot on the stove will cause boiling water to pour onto our bodies, burning us severely. We learn not to walk out into a busy street, because we'll be run over by a car and die. In their efforts to be loving, our parents teach us about the many dangers and fears associated with living in this world. We begin to sense danger all around us—and we begin to lose faith in a safe, loving world.

Then, at some point between the ages of two and six, we all experience a single, dramatic event—one that will define the remaining years of our lives. Before this event, we were just ongoing expressions of our natural Selves who did not worry about the definition of "who we were," did not worry about how we were acting, and did not care about what others thought of us. We never even thought or considered whether or not we were lovable. We never worried about defining ourselves as persons; we did not worry about what someone else saw in us.

No, those thoughts just never entered our minds. But then an event occurred, one we interpreted as telling us that "we are not lovable," one that we interpreted as "we are not smart enough," or we are not pretty enough, that we are not *something* enough to be worthy of someone else's love.

> You're aware that this life experience began in the womb; you found it comfortable there. It was warm and it was secure. You floated through life. You were fed, and it was a form of heavenly experience.
>
> Then one day, those muscles started pushing you outward and you were reluctant to leave that comfortable environment—though you had no memory of that experience.
>
> And then, during the next six, seven, eight years, most of the attitudes you presently have were formed.[5]
>
> — Stretton Smith

For some of us this event occurs as part of an innocuous, innocent situation, or a set of circumstances most outsiders would never recognize as being significant. Sometimes this event results from a more dramatic event, like verbal, emotional, physical, or sexual abuse, or as an event that can be interpreted as such.

Whenever this event occurs, we interpret the situation as evidence that we are not lovable, that we are not worthy of someone else's loving us. For some reason, we seem to automatically believe this interpretation completely, without question. Immediately this event shakes us down to our foundation; we lose touch with our faith in the person we were only moments before. And when this happens, we absolutely know that we're the only person on the planet that feels this way. We feel that if anyone knew how we really felt, they would validate our worst fear possible: that, indeed, we are not lovable or are not worthy of another person's love.

We then create identities for ourselves based on this interpretation that we are not worthy of being loved, that we are not lovable. We create behaviors that are specifically designed to demonstrate to the world that we, indeed, are worthy and are lovable. We expend tremendous amounts of energy overcompensating for these perceived flaws in our design.

We may become self-absorbed, overwhelmed, and desperate in our attempts to prove to the world that we are indeed lovable. When someone does love us, we refuse to believe him or her. We believe he is only feeling that way because of the identity we created and not because he loves the person we really are. We live in complete and utter terror that another person on this planet will learn our terrible secret, that "we are not lovable, not worthy of having another person love us." We go to almost any length to keep this secret to ourselves, to hide this terrible life flaw—pretending, overcompensating.

This type of event and the related interpretation that follows occurs *for every single person on the planet at one time or another, in one form or another, to one extent or another.* Everyone goes through this at some level, sometimes in a manner that's barely noticeable in our lives, although for many others of us this phenomenon drives our every waking moment's behavior and consciousness.

Many of us never were aware of what happened that triggered all this. We might not have much insight into what is currently happening; we only know that our lives are not working, and we don't ever feel at peace with ourselves or with the world. Some of us are painfully aware of some or all of this process; we just don't know how to transcend the traps that our beliefs have created for us. However, it is also true that nothing alters the fact that this event and related interpretation are driven by the soul *as an integral step on the path to enlightenment.*

As we saw in the first chapter, these stories and their related interpretations are quite diverse. But everyone on the planet lives through the same experience. **Everyone on this planet experiences at least one defining event in their early childhood, then creates an interpretation that they are not lovable and begin to live their lives based on this belief system. This sequence is part of the Grand Design.**

Let me introduce you to "Mike," who will be sharing his experiences to illustrate several of this book's key

Over our lifetime, in collaboration with family and friends, we have woven a story about ourselves that defines who we are. The ego cannot be understood or expressed except in relation to an audience, and this audience's responses— real or imagined—continually shaping our telling of the story. We do not consciously and deliberately figure out what narratives to tell and how to tell them. For the most part, we don't spin our tales: They spin us.[6]

— Daniel C. Matt, Ph.D.

principles and ideas. Mike has graciously volunteered to share this journey with us, by talking about his life experiences and his spiritual journey. Mike is a fairly typical man in his early forties; he stands about 5-feet, 11-inches tall and is of average weight and build. Mike grew up in a small town and now lives in a large city. He fell in love and married his high school sweetheart, Christine, and they now have two teenage children (one son named Thomas and one daughter named Sarah) and a dog named Adidas.

On the outside, it may appear that Mike has achieved everything he dreamed of as a child; yet beneath his "surface" this is hardly the case. Mike has very few friends. His relationships with his wife and children are often strained. Mike is virtually closed off from the world, he does not allow himself to be vulnerable or open to anyone, including his family. Whenever given the opportunity to share himself, Mike shrinks away into the shadows and avoids contact with anyone.

Mike's friends and family have come to accept Mike as he is. After years of attempting to draw out Mike, they all have given up and decided to just leave him alone. But his wife feels strongly resentful and sad that she has never really been able to let Mike know how much she loves him. Mike never opens up enough for anyone, even his wife, to get close; whenever someone tries to show Mike how much he's cared for, he closes up even more.

Mike has felt a deep sense of loss and loneliness for most of his life, and this feeling has grown progressively worse over the last several years. Late at night, in moments of deep introspection, Mike will admit to himself that he feels like he is not a lovable person. He feels that if anyone found out his deep dark secret, that person would confront him with just how unlovable he is and this would be unbearable.

Mike has never found any sense of peace of mind or heart. He has always lived in a near-panic state, fearing someone would find out about his secret. Mike sees everyone around him as living lives that seem filled with loving relationships, fun, and joy. Yet for most of his life Mike has never felt that this is something he would ever have.

But finally, after living forty plus years of loneliness and pain, Mike has decided that he is ready for a change—ready to find a way out of his prison. So Mike has graciously volunteered to take this journey with us, hoping to discover how to turn his life around to fill all his dreams. I will tell you that Mike is a composite character who represents some of me and parts of several close friends of mine who have also taken the journey to Self-love. And I think that if you look carefully enough, you, too, might be able to find at least a little bit of yourself in Mike and his journey.

So we've asked Mike to share his childhood experiences, along with why and how he believes those experiences have contributed to his current situation. He says,

*I was born in a small Midwest town, the middle child of three children (I have an older sister and a younger brother). I did pretty well in grade school and participated in several Little League baseball and football teams during my youth. I think to the casual observer my family would look like almost every other family in America. I started out as a happy, outgoing child, but then became increasingly shy and withdrawn.*

*Behind the doors of my house, my father was an alcoholic who often came home at night drunk and angry with his lot in life. My father would take his disappointments and frustrations out on his children, and seemed to mostly target his middle child, me. He often told me how dumb I was. He would tell me I wasn't smart enough to be successful in life, and then he would slap me around. Any excuse seemed to trigger my father's anger, resulting in the evenings being filled with angry tirades aimed primarily at me. At first, I thought he was treating me this way because I was being a "bad boy." But as the years went by and this abuse continued, I began to accept the perspective that I really wasn't smart; that I really **wouldn't** ever amount to anything because I was so unlovable.*

*Deep inside, I began to feel ashamed of myself. I began to feel like a failure. I began to feel that God must have created me with some deep inherent flaw that made me (and me alone) so unlovable. More than anything else, I wanted (like most young boys do) to be loved and respected by my father; yet all I heard from him was what a miserable person I was. I became thoroughly convinced I was a failure as a person, that I was unlovable. This belief left me feeling filled with shame and scared to death that if someone else learned this "truth" about me they would also not love me.*

*I became convinced over the years that I was a complete failure, doomed to live a life of mediocrity at best. To compensate for these feelings, I became increasingly withdrawn and quiet. I always wanted to be a doctor when I was young, but I came to believe I wasn't smart enough for that profession. I didn't think I could ever get through medical school; and even if I did, no one would come to me for treatment because I was such a miserable person. So I gave up that dream fairly early on.*

*As I progressed through school, I began to like math because I could be alone with these problems. With math, there was no reason to reveal myself or to be around people. I ended up taking accounting in college and went on to become an accountant. I now often live at work with my computer rather than living with people. This has allowed me to avoid dealing with people, and to keep enough distance so people would never learn my terrible secret—that I was unlovable.*

So Mike avoids almost any possibility of intimate conversation, avoids spending time alone with other people, even his family. His wife, Christine, has resigned herself to Mike's habits and has stepped into the role of the parent and center of the family. As many times as she has reached out and attempted to invite Mike into the family, she has been rebuffed. Finally, Christine just gave up and like everyone else just allows Mike to sit on the sidelines of life and watch.

But after forty years of lonely, passionless, painful life, Mike is ready for a change. Mike is ready to take the journey to find a different way to live. Mike is ready to begin to find a way to feel good about himself, to feel safe enough about himself to open up and share his feelings with the people he loves the most. Mike is ready to take a hard look at his life and do whatever is necessary to find some peace of mind and heart.

Deep inside Mike loves his wife, his children, and his family very much, and he's completely frustrated by his inability to tell them and show them how he feels. Mike has finally begun to understand that he is wasting his life, he is losing out on all the love that life has to offer. So, now Mike is ready to make the journey from pain and struggle to joy and love.

The type of event and the related interpretation Mike suffered happen every day to people all around the world. They are not a "wrong," they are not a "right," they just *are*. Something happens in all our lives and helps generate a belief system based on the feeling that "I'm not lovable."

Sometimes a simple comment from an adult generates this interpretation; sometimes it comes as the result of abuse in some form; sometimes it's the result of simple teasing by our young peers; and sometimes we even generate our own interpretations without outside influences. The soul seeks out whatever source is available at the right time to generate the interpretation that "I am not lovable."

Sometimes the input is severe, such as with physical or sexual abuse. Sometimes the input is fairly innocent, as simple as a parent punishing a child in an appropriate manner for his or her disobedience. Sometimes the input comes from somewhere in between these extremes.

But however the input comes, the soul seeks whatever input is available to create this interpretation. As you will soon learn, **it's part of the soul's divine purpose to find a "reason" to generate the interpretation of the input signifying "I'm not lovable."** Then, based on that interpretation, we proceed with our lives based on the belief that we are not lovable. We then create our entire lives, our entire identities based on this belief.

Yes, it happens to every person on this planet at one time, to one extent or another. Yet when it's happening to you, you feel guilty and ashamed that you are "not a lovable person." But there's hope, for this is all part of the Grand Design because it serves to move the soul along the Path to Enlightenment. Now let's take a look at this Path, for we shall soon see how even the interpretation "I'm not lovable" serves towards our achieving Enlightenment.

## Your divine purpose

**Universally, every major spiritual and religious teaching tells us that our divine purpose on this planet is to experience God.** We are instructed that our divine purpose is to experience the Spirit inside each and every one of us. But exactly how do we do this? Again, I've heard very few teachers explain this clearly enough to make sense to me.

> When I was a child, I spake as a child, I understood as a child, I thought as a child: but when I became a man, I put away childish things.
>
> — *First Letter to the Corinthians* 13:11

To try to understand what the great teachers have said, let's go back to the basics and start by looking at our definitions of God. While I was growing up in a small town in West Texas, I had a vision of God as a large man with a pot belly and a long, flowing white beard and mustache. He sat on His throne, in front of the calendar (my version back then of the Divine Plan), directing each of us in our daily lives as we lived out our destiny.

One day while playing on the school playground, I broke my leg. I thought that God had looked down that day at His calendar, seen that breaking my leg was part of the Divine Plan, and willed that my leg be broken (as if He had pulled on, then let go of, a puppet's string). But as I grew into adulthood this vision seemed to make less and less sense to me. I couldn't understand why God should look so much like Santa Claus. I also didn't understand why God should be physically out of shape. I mean, if anyone could afford to buy a health club membership or own a Bow-Flex®, it was God. As I grew up and matured, my vision of God did, too. So I began to look for a different perspective on God.

> Jesus gave us a simple commandment, "Love one another" (*Gospel of John* 15:17). The Jews follow love's way: "You shall love the Lord your God with all your heart, and with all your soul, and with all your might" (*Book of Deuteronomy* 6:5). Hindus likewise give allegiance to love: "Show love to all creatures and thou wilt be happy, for when thou lovest all things, thou lovest the Lord, for he is in all" (Tinsu Das Hindu spiritualist). It is also true of the Buddhists: "As a mother, even at the risk of her own life, protects her son, her only son, so let him cultivate love with measure toward all beings" (*The Sutta Nipata*).[7]
>
> — Jim Rosemergy

### Your divine purpose is to experience God.

Once I was fully grown up and had begun reading extensively through the many teachings of the world's religions, I discovered that every religious and spiritual teaching since the beginning of time has used the image of "love" to teach us about God. All these teachings share the same message: "God is love." That this is not a great message, I think nobody can seriously argue. Yet how do we apply this message to our everyday lives? How do I make my day, my *life*, better through these teachings?

Jesus provided us with the answer. Besides being a great spiritual teacher, Jesus was also a great teacher of human psychology. One of his best students, John, the "beloved" disciple, shared his rare insight into the human mind in his letter, known as *First John*:

> Beloved, let us love one another: for love is of God; and every one that loveth is born of God, and knoweth God.

> He that loveth not knoweth not God; for God is love (1 *Gospel of John* 4:7-8).

His message is quite clear. **God is love. If you want to know God, then know love. If you don't know love, then you don't know God. To know God, you must express love in your life.** Only through this means, Jesus taught, can you actually experience God's presence in your life.

John went on to teach more about his master's message in the same letter: "God is love; and he that dwelleth in love dwelleth in God, and God in him" (1 *Gospel of John* 4:16). There is no better way to experience God than to feel that God "dwelleth" in you. You can literally experience the presence of God in your life when you open your heart and share the love that is inherent within you.

Now, these teachings don't suggest "God is *loving*," because that would imply that God has the capability of being un-loving. They consistently have taught us that God is love; God is the very energy of love pulsating

> God is beyond relative good and evil. He is the absolute Good.[8]
>
> — Swami Prabhavananda

through the Universe. Love is the life force pulsating throughout the Universe; love is the healing energy flowing through our bodies. Furthermore, love is the greatest power, and love is more than capable of overcoming fear, pain, and suffering wherever they may be found. Yes, Jesus taught us that to experience God we need to experience love.

At first when I read that "God is love" and that to know God you must express love, I thought, "Of course." But further contemplation left me wondering, *What does this really mean in my everyday life?* So I read some more and studied some more. Eventually I came to realize the beauty and the logic of John's statement. Reading from the Christian New Testament in 1 *John* 4:6, *"We're of God." If God gave birth to us,* I thought, *then it makes sense that we have within us all the same characteristics as God.* In the *Torah*, the *Book of Genesis* 1:27 explains that this is because, "God created man in his own image, in the image of God created he him . . ." [9] **Because God is love, and God created us in His image, then our divine nature must also be love. When we express our divine nature, our divine essence, then**

**we will experience our divinity.** Absolutely beautiful, simple, elegant—and the Truth.

This Truth is stated outside of the Judeo-Christian tradition as well. Sufism is an ancient set of mystical teachings of Islam. The Sufis also support this perspective of God being the energy of love. Furthermore, they teach that expressing love in all aspects of your life is the path to experiencing God. The Sufis use the term baraka for blessing, as in, "May you receive more blessings or love in your life." This term can easily be translated into spiritual energy, in other words, "May you receive more spiritual energy in your life." You can also read this to mean, "May you receive more love in your life."

When the scribes (and the high priests of Judea during Jesus's time) asked Jesus to define the most important commandment of all, Jesus's reply was simple: Let there be love. Jesus said, "Love God with all thy heart and soul," and since we are all one with God, that means that you should love everyone with all your heart and soul. Jesus went on to clarify this statement when he spoke further: "Love your neighbor as thyself." So, besides loving God and everyone else on this planet, we should also love our Selves in order to experience our divinity. As we have all heard said more than once, you can't love someone else until you love your Self first. To become an ongoing expression of love, you must first learn to love your Self.

Which is the first commandment of all?

And Jesus answered him, *"The first of all the commandments is, Hear, O Israel; The Lord our God is one Lord:*

*And thou shalt love the Lord thy God with all thy heart, and with all thy soul, and with all thy mind, and with all thy strength: this is the first commandment.*

*And the second is like, namely this, Thou shalt love thy neighbour as thyself. There is none other commandment greater than these."*

— *Gospel of Mark* 12:28-31

Once again, these teachings are consistent across almost all religious and spiritual teachings. **If God is the energy of love, and our divine purpose is to experience God in our lives, then our divine purpose is to experience love in all aspects of our lives. Experiencing love in all aspects of your life starts with and includes loving your Self.**

### God is love; God is the energy of love.

But, in the midst of all this madness in the world, how can man possibly express love in all aspects of our lives? What does it mean that if we know love, we know God? Does this really tell us how to love during our real lives? Jesus taught us that, when we express our love, we experience

God. This seems logical to me. Since God is love, when we express love we are expressing God. **Whatever we express is what we experience. So the only way to experience God, or love, is to express love.** We experience what we express. We only experience the emotions and feelings we are sharing or expressing.

## We experience what we express.

I have heard that what people really want is to be loved. But humans don't experience love merely when someone else loves us. The human mind is not capable of experiencing someone else's emotions or feelings. We only experience our own emotions. For example, man does not have an experience called "being loved," we only have an experience called "loving."

> Beloved, let us love one another: for love is of God; and every one that loveth is born of God, and knoweth God.
>
> He that loveth not knoweth not God; for God is love.
>
> — *Gospel of John* 4:7-8

We all have probably had people in our lifetime tell us that they love us, yet we can't feel that love in our hearts. The moment they are not around and reminding us of their love, whatever feeling we had dissipates. On the other hand, we certainly can feel the love pulsating through our own bodies whenever we are actively demonstrating our love towards someone else. When we open our hearts and share ourselves in great depth, we experience the emotion of love throughout our entire bodies. When we open our hearts and do something special that expresses love for another person, we feel the warmth as it spreads from our hearts throughout our entire bodies. Every time we relive those memories of our expression of love, we feel those same emotions and sensations gently coursing through our systems.

The human mind cannot experience what another person is expressing. We can see evidence of this as we look at our movie stars, music stars, politicians, and famous athletes. Most of these people are idolized and loved by thousands, if not millions. Many people pay their hard-earned money to buy the

> . . . [L]ife is a matter of developing or unfolding from within, that life is not something to get, but something to express.[10]
>
> — Eric Butterworth

tabloids just to keep up with celebrities' every move; we watch *Entertainment Tonight* to find out what has happened in their lives. Knowing their favorite restaurants somehow enhances our lives—or so many people believe.

Yet this small segment of the population (the movie stars, the professional athletes, etc.) suffers from depression, drug and alcohol use, and suicide attempts at a rate far higher than almost any other population segment. Why? I believe it's because most of the stars don't know whom they can trust with their heart and their love. They must always wonder if the people in their lives are offering their support and love merely because of their fame and fortune, not because of who they are as persons. Because they don't feel safe opening their hearts, sharing their love, and expressing themselves without the need to feel guarded, they lack the opportunity to experience themselves as loving. Because they don't experience themselves as their natural expressions of love, they become depressed and frustrated and lonely. I believe it's this loneliness and frustration that drives so many of them to alcoholism, drug abuse, and suicide as escapes.

You see, they don't *feel* the idolatry and the love of the masses; for they can't experience the emotions and feelings of their fans. They are only capable of experiencing what they express, and often they feel as if they have to hide or withhold their own, true expressions of love. So being loved by millions can't save them; only feeling strong enough and safe enough to express their love can possibly save them from their emotional imprisonment. And if it's their inability to feel safe to express the love inside themselves that causes so much of their frustration and loneliness, it's our same inability to feel safe to love our Selves, or to love others, which also causes so much of our own frustration and loneliness.

**Our souls deeply desire to express themselves as loving.** I think you will see this fact illustrated by a couple of examples. When a person sees a young kitten or a tiny puppy, he naturally wants to reach down and cuddle it. When we see very young babies, we want to hold them and express our love towards them (even if that just means holding a baby for a moment and looking into its eyes— that's a form of being loving).

(Jesus said),

*For who does now know self does not know anything, but whoever knows self already has acquired knowledge about the depth of the Universe.* [11]
— *The Book of Thomas* 1:6

In both cases we feel we can reach out and express the soul's natural expressions in this way, because in each of these instances we feel completely safe. After all, what could be safer to an adult than a very small kitten or puppy, or a newborn baby? It's when we are around other full-grown people, especially people we don't know well, that we often feel fearful. When we are unsure whether or not we can trust people, we don't feel safe to open and share our Selves and make our Selves vulnerable. Can you see how fears like these cause so much frustration and pain in the world?

One reason being in the midst of these fears causes us so much frustration is this: *The human mind is only capable of experiencing one primary emotion at a time.* Nobody can be actively and intensely experiencing deep love for another person and at the same time be consciously hating that person. Man is only capable of experiencing either fear or experiencing love at any given time. Man can't experience both emotions at the same time. Jesus shared one of his psychological insights during his Sermon on the Mount, recorded in the *Gospel of Matthew 5:22-24:*

> We cannot love God and hate our neighbour. If we really love God, we will find him in everyone; so how can we hate another? If we harm anyone, we harm ourselves; if we help another, we help ourselves.[12]
>
> — Swami Prabhavanananda

> *That whosoever is angry with his brother without a cause shall be in danger of the judgment: and whosoever shall say to his brother, Raca, shall be in danger of the council: but whosoever shall say, Thou fool, shall be in danger of hell fire.*
>
> *Therefore if thou bring thy gift to the altar, and there rememberest that thy brother hath ought against thee;*
>
> *Leave there thy gift before the altar, and go thy way; first be reconciled to thy brother, and then come and offer thy gift.*

In other words, he said you can't go into the altar of your heart while you are consumed with anger. We must first clean up our anger before we can return our hearts to the love that is the essence of God. You can only be expressing one emotion at a time, and it is your choice which one you are involved with.

**Our souls' greatest desire is to experience our divinity, the love that is inherent in our hearts. That is what all of us were programmed to seek when we were first created. Yet when we are in the midst of experiencing our fears, we can't express our love. Our divine purpose, our souls' deepest desire, is then frustrated. When this happens, our souls and our bodies then transmit messages out to us that "say" we are not fulfilling our divine purpose. These messages may be in the form of loneliness, frustration, stress, pain, and erosion of our health.**

The great teacher, Jesus, specifically taught that when you express love, you experience God. When you experience God, you fulfill your divine purpose. That makes perfect sense. God is love. You experience what you express. Therefore, if you are expressing love, then you will be experiencing God. And what better way to know God than to experience God?

**Your divine purpose is to become an expression of love.**

Your True Nature as a divine being is one of love. When you express the inherent love within your heart, you will quickly begin to recognize the rewards of love's expression throughout your entire life. Dr. Dean Ornish, one of the world's top cardiologists, made his name in the medical field by teaching that diet and exercise can have positive effects on heart disease. While researching in this field, Dr. Ornish went on to make an even greater discovery. He noted that a great many medical research studies over the past 100 years clearly indicated that the factor that most promotes health is being in a relationship in which you are freely expressing your love.

> It may be of a passing interest to note that Jesus used the word *sclerocardia* twice in (*Gospel of*) *Mark* in referring the hardening of the heart. Once, He referred to hardened hearts sealed against mercy and forgiveness.[13]
>
> — Stretton Smith

Dr. Ornish summarized his findings after reviewing medical studies over the last two centuries in his book, *Love & Survival: The Scientific Basis for the Healing Power of Intimacy:*

> I'm not aware of any other factor in medicine—not diet, not smoking, not exercise, not stress, not genetics, not drugs, not surgery—that has a greater impact on our quality of life, incidence, and premature death from all causes (other than love).[14]

Furthermore, it has become common knowledge (and has been statistically verified) that married people do live longer than single people. I believe this is because married people have found other individuals with whom they feel safe to share themselves at depth; they have found particular persons with whom they can unconditionally share their love. The same holds true with people and pets. It has also been scientifically proven that people with pets have lower blood pressure and live longer. Why? They live longer because they have safe objects toward which they can express their heartfelt love, confident that their pets will return their love unconditionally.

We are designed to experience fear during our lives in order for us to be able to fully understand and experience love in great depth. Our natural states as divine beings are ones of love. When we express ourselves divinely, we are expressing our Selves at the highest level of consciousness. When we express the

> Disease and health, like circumstances, are rooted in thought. Sickly thoughts will express themselves through a sickly body. Thoughts of fear have been known to kill a man as speedily as a bullet, and they are continually killing thousands of people just as surely though less rapidly. The people who live in fear of disease are the people who get it.[15]
>
> — James Allen

inherent love we have in our hearts, we rejuvenate our immune systems and build positive expressions of our health. These expressions of our health rebuild the cells within our bodies, send forth renewing energy to every organ and appendage, and "turbo-charge" our immune systems. Sharing the love you naturally have in your heart causes you to live longer, free from sickness and even accidents—that's a scientifically proven fact.

Although it may seem somewhat contrary to many of our daily experiences, our natural state as divine beings is to live our lives filled with abundance and prosperity. When we express our Selves from states of love, abundance and prosperity naturally flow to you (whatever abundance and prosperity mean to you as an individual). Wealth, in all its states (material wealth, vitality and health, great relationships, peace of heart, peace of mind, etc.), naturally flows to the energy of love. It's when we express our Selves from fear that we literally shut the door to that flow of abundance and experience poverty instead.

> Clinicians have the impression that increasing self-esteem seems to slow the progress of the disease (human immunodeficiency virus). This leads me to speculate that VIP (vasoactive intestinal peptide) might be the hormonal manifestation of self-love, just as endorphins are the underlying mechanisms for bliss and bonding.[16]
>
> — Candace B. Pert, Ph.D.

Our natural state is to be loving and generous persons. As such, our greatest desire as humans is to express the love that is inherent in each of us. When we adopt a belief system based on a lack of Self-love, then this heartfelt desire becomes frustrated. Again, you can't love another person until you truly love your Self. So, as long as we hold onto belief systems that lack Self-love, our ability to experience our divinity will be frustrated and denied to us, and it will seem as if we were destined to experience this frustration and pain.

If our natural state as divine beings is to express our Selves as love, and in doing so to experience God, then why do we spend so much of our lives expressing fear? If love is who we really are, then why did God "invent" fear, and thus pain and suffering? At first, His doing so does not seem to make sense. Only when we look a little deeper and view these issues in a larger context can we answer these questions logically.

Our natural divine state is to be expressions of love, experiencing vitality and health, experiencing loving relationships, and experiencing

> If you look underneath your depression, you'll find anger. Look under your anger, and you'll find sadness. And under sadness is the root of it all, what's really masquerading all the while—fear.[17]
>
> — Carolyn Stearns

abundance and prosperity. Yet each of us has experienced that first moment of insecurity that generated the "interpretation" that led to our lack of Self-love. Living from belief in this interpretation, we all have built our lives based on such belief and such fears, and we have therefore generated lives filled with pain and suffering. But if our naturally divine state is to live as expressions of love, does it make sense that every one of us should live so much of our lives experiencing fear?

Because every single person on the planet has this experience, we can only surmise that it's part of the Grand Design. But why would any Higher Power want us each to build a major part of our life on fear? If this Higher Power were our Heavenly Father, as some religions teach, wouldn't this Higher Power want us to live our lives based on love and the experience of joy? Didn't Jesus tell us that part of one of the two most important commandments is to love ourselves? The answer is yes. God, our Higher Power, does want us to experience lives based on love and joy. But in order to fully experience love, we must also fully experience its opposite, fear. Let me explain.

Modern science has proven that all energy, and thus all matter, in the Universe emanated from a single source (called the Point of Singularity), during what is known as the Big Bang. This energy is divine and pulses throughout Universe as the substance underlying all matter throughout the entire Universe. We refer to this energy as God, or as the energy of love.

Everything in the Universe was and is generated from this divine energy, so this energy is the foundation for everything. All the latest findings in quantum mechanics, relativity physics, and astrophysics have proven that only one form of energy pervades the Universe, and it is the very foundation of all underlying matter. No second force, no other energy source exists. Only one type of energy flows through the Universe. Yet in order to experience this energy, our souls must generate the experience of a source of energy that is other than the energy shaped as love, and this is the experience of fear.

Fear, in and of itself, is not real. The underlying foundation of all fears is falsehood. That's why some have taught that fear is really an acronym for *F*alse *E*vidence *A*ppearing *R*eal. **The human mind can't distinguish between an actual and imagined event; they both seem very real to our minds.** Humans take in sensory input on an equal basis from both our imaginations and our five senses. So the soul grabs hold of false belief and then creates the experience of fear, so that the soul can fully experience its opposite, love.

Love and the energy of love are the only real aspects in the Universal construct. Yet the experience of fear can seem very real. The basis of the fear is not real, but the experience of the fear seems very real. (Good news: We will begin to see later in this book how love can overcome all fears.)

The human mind can only understand particular things in relation to each other. **We only understand one experience in <u>contrast</u> to another. It is the contrast that allows us to have an experience.** If there were only light, with no darkness, the human mind would not be able to grasp the concept of light. If there were only love, the human mind would not be able to experience fear. If there were only fear, the human mind could not experience love. If there were only tall, the human mind would be incapable of grasping the concept of short. The human mind requires separate points of reference, or contrasts, to understand anything. Therefore, our souls generate contrasting experiences from which they can grow. Let's examine this principle step-by-step.

> Being and non-being create each other.
>
> Difficult and easy support each other.
>
> Long and short define each other.
>
> High and low depend on each other.
>
> Before and after follow each other.[18]
>
> — *Tao Te Ching*, Chapter 2

The human mind only generates experience when it recognizes, through its five senses, change. The human mind detects change (on any level), and it is from this change that the mind generates experiences. If anything in your life remains static—the same day after day—you become numb to this and even cease to see that it is static.

> We all perceive the world by observing the differences in our sensory fields, such as varieties of tastes, texture, color, etc.[19]
>
> — Gregory Bateson, M.D.

For example, you may get in your car every day and drive to the same place (either to work or to some other destination) by the same route. Because virtually all the scenery you experience (through any of your senses, not just visually) remains the same day after day, after a while you cease to even notice it. When you are driving to work every day, you don't notice your surroundings (hopefully, though, you still notice the cars on the road!)

If someone were to tear down a building on your route that had been standing for years, you would certainly notice the new view, and it would register in your mind: "Hey, they tore down that old mini-mart on the corner."

But sometimes we even become so numb to "same-old, same-old," everyday experiences, we go through the motions in a kind of "auto-pilot" and don't even remember doing them. Have you ever driven to work and then, while walking into the building from the parking lot, thought, "Hey, how did I get here?" That was because your mind only registers change. Without change, your mind would experience nothing.

This phenomenon explains why people who live next to noisy railroad or mass-transit lines eventually "tune out" the noise. I have a friend who lives in New York City. Her apartment is fairly close to one of the elevated subway train tracks. On a regular basis, you can hear the train as it roars down the tracks outside. Yet because she has lived there for so many years, she no longer hears the trains at all. One day I mentioned the noise to her, and she looked at me with this puzzled look and said, "Is the noise that bad? I've stopped even hearing it at all." The reason her mind no longer hears it is that it has become a constant in her life, and she has grown numb to the constant noise.

This friend and I were talking recently about this concept, and it took her a moment to understand what I was saying. Her eyes lit up then, and she told me that immediately after the September 11, 2001, tragedy, subway service for the train

> The Tao doesn't take sides;
>
> it gives birth to both good and evil.[20]
>
> — *Tao Te Ching*, Chapter 5

that ran past her apartment was suspended. She said, "I suddenly noticed a very loud silence all day, and it really bothered me. For some reason, it felt so—so surreal and eerie."

Why was this so? Because her mind had grown so used to the noise from the train on its regular schedule, she had ceased to even notice it. Then when the trains did not run, her mind recognized the change. When something changed from the ordinary, she immediately recognized it, and only then did her mind notice and experience the change.

You see another example of this concept when you try to cook live lobsters. One way to cook the lobster is to pour the water into your cooking pot, turn the stove on, and wait until the water boils. If you then attempt to put live lobsters into that boiling water, the lobsters will definitely struggle and fight to avoid being placed in the pot. On the other hand, if you place the lobsters in the water and then turn up the stove, slowly raising the water temperature, the lobsters won't react. They will sit in the water, not noticing the gently increasing heat, and will cook with-

> According to the *Vedanta*, there are two kinds of knowledge.
>
> The first, the lower, consists of academic knowledge, such as science and philosophy.
>
> Even knowledge of the scriptures is considered lower knowledge.
>
> The second, the higher knowledge, is the immediate perception of God.[21]
>
> — Swami Prabhavananda

out struggling. With the first method, the lobsters notice the change in their environment and react strongly. The second way, the lobsters don't notice the slow change and won't react. The same holds true for people. We only experience life and its situations if we notice changes in our lives.

Fish don't "experience" water because it is the environment they live in every day. We, similarly, don't experience air, because we move through and breathe air every moment of every day. Now, I am not saying we don't experience wind, but that's the change in the force of air. I'm talking about air itself. We don't experience air because we live in the midst of air every moment of every day.

However, imagine (don't worry, I'll never really do it!) that I took your head and held it under water for three minutes, or long enough that you were sure you were going to pass out and drown. Then imagine that I allowed you to raise your head out of the water so you could breathe again. At that moment you would fully experience air.

Our divine purpose on this planet is to experience ourselves expressing love, and through this expression, we will experience our divinity. If you were born on this planet and only expressed love from the first day of your birth until the last breath of your life, you would not *experience* love. So your expression of love would be similar to the air you live in each day, because you would not have the experience of love, not having experienced its opposite. Just as you wouldn't hear the train that roared by your apartment every day of your life, you wouldn't experience the energy of love flowing through your life.

Our souls have to create change in our lives so we experience life and love. **In order to experience our Selves expressing love, our souls create the experiences of our Selves expressing fear. Our souls search for any reason that will cause us to generate the belief system that "we are not lovable," so we will then begin to express our Selves as fear.** You see, our souls had to find reasons for us to believe we needed to protect our Selves—reasons for us to hide the persons we really are inside.

"I am the Eternal and there is nothing else. I make light and create darknesss. I make peace and create evil" (*Book of Isaiah* 45:6-7). The infinite source of light withdraws and darkness is created. The infinite source of peace (*shalom,* from the root *shalaim* meaning whole, complete) withdraws and evil (lack of perfection) is created.[22]

— Gerald L. Schroeder, Ph.D.

So our souls all used the most convenient "reason" available during our childhood: the belief that "we are not lovable." Once we adopted this belief system, we naturally generated our entire identities, as well as a great deal of our lives, based on the fear that someone might find out our terrible secret. Of course, this "secret" (that "we are unlovable") is a lie. Each one of us is an incredibly divine being merely because he or she exists as a human being. Some of us just have a harder time than others demonstrating that we are incredible persons.

## The soul seeks a basis to generate a lack of Self-love, which serves the higher Purpose of causing the soul to experience fear.

**Our souls need to create the false belief of fear in order to understand and fully experience our Selves expressing love.** For this reason, until we heal this false belief, we will believe anything negative about our Selves before we believe anything good. We will believe the negative because the soul requires us to experience fear. And only once we have thoroughly experienced lives filled with fear will we then be ready to experience lives filled with love.

The great Taoist teacher Lao-Tzu taught this about these fear-love contrasts created by the Universe: "That which lets now the dark, now the light appear is *Tao.*"[23] God's essence contains both attributes: darkness and light, love and fear. This theme also appears in Lao-Tzu's metaphor of the mountain: ". . . where first light shines on one side of the mountain and darkness the other." Have you noticed: darkness and light seemingly exchange sides as the sun transverses across the sky? This was the original meaning of the now "familiar" words *yin* and *yang* (they have since taken on many new and diverse meanings). This *yin/yang* concept refers to the duality that exists throughout the Universe, in which there are always two sides to each situation. It is this duality that allows us to experience life.

So if God/Spirit is absolute Good, and if God is all-powerful, then why is God allowing so much suffering on this planet? Why doesn't God merely will away all pain and suffering? If we are Children of this all-powerful God, and if God's love is so much greater than our ability to understand, then why does God allow His/Her Children to suffer so much pain? If God is love, and our divine purpose is to experience God, then why doesn't God will us to experience only love? These are questions I have wrestled with for most of my life (perhaps you have, too) as I've searched for spiritual teachings I could subscribe to.

I believe that the only reason God, who is all-powerful and all loving, would allow His/Her Children to experience so much pain and suffering is because this pain and suffering must serve a greater purpose. The pain and suffering must be part of the Divine Plan, the Grand Design.

We may also logically assume that this pain must be part of the Grand Design because everyone on the planet experiences the same phenomenon. And the sole reason we do experience so much fear, and then generate lives of pain and suffering, is so we can afterwards experience love deeply.

## We must experience fear in order to experience love.

But if this is true, then we should find "spiritual precedent" for these teachings about this duality throughout many ancient spiritual and religious teachings. If we take a fresh look at the very old story of Adam and Eve, we do indeed find such a precedent.

I'm sure you recall the story: Adam and Eve were both living lives filled with bliss and joy in the Garden of Eden, where the sun shined every day and the climate was always moderate. Food and shelter they had in plenty, and they enjoyed a veritable feast of fresh fruits and vegetables always readily available. They didn't have a care in the world; their life together was perfect.

Yet even so, something was missing: They had no intellectual or emotional or spiritual stimulation. Without this stimulation, they could experience no real growth or development. They could not really appreciate this Nirvana, because it was all they knew. They had no contrasts against which to experience the joy in their lives.

So they sought to "be as gods, knowing good and evil" (*Book of Genesis* 3:4). I would suggest that Adam and Eve were living in the consciousness of love and abundance, represented by the Garden of Eden. But their souls desired to know the experience of love, and therefore they had to learn the experience of fear ("knowing good and evil"). So they ate of the tree of knowledge. Then what happened? We find out from reading from the *Book of Genesis* 3:5-10:

> If men had been forbidden to make porridge of camel's dung, they would have done it, saying that they would not have been forbidden to do it unless there had been some good in it. [24]
>
> — The Prophet Muhammad

> And the eyes of them both were opened, and they knew that they were naked; and they sewed fig leaves together, and made themselves aprons. And they heard the voice of the LORD God walking in the garden in the cool of the day: and Adam and his wife hid themselves from the presence of the LORD God amongst the trees of the garden. And the LORD God called unto Adam, and said unto him, Where art thou? And he said, I heard thy voice in the garden, and *I was afraid, because I was naked; and I hid myself. (emphasis added)*

Once they ate of the tree of knowledge "the eyes of them both were opened" and they immediately became "afraid," self-conscious; they were ashamed of their bodies, so they "hid." They immediately started feeling insecure and unlovable, so they began to hide themselves from God. They "sewed fig leaves together"—made themselves clothes—because they felt uncomfortable about their bodies, whereas moments before they had been secure as they were. Then when God came looking for them, they hid because they were "afraid." *This is the first moment in human*

FIVE SECRETS TO SELF-LOVE

*history in which it's recorded that man expressed any fear—and the first moment in human history in which man is reported to have experienced feelings of a lack of Self-love.*

I believe this entire story has been misinterpreted for years, along lines I will describe shortly. What I believe this story is telling us is that, to fully understand the experience of love (which is to understand the experience of God), we must first experience fear.

Some top biblical scholars suggest that the Bible presents, in essence, a series of metaphors for the spiritual journey each of us makes through the course of our lives. Each story describes a different segment or portion of our lives as we travel through the many experiences in our spiritual maturation process. Each phase of this trip represents our consciousnesses as we move towards greater spiritual awareness.

In this view, the Garden of Eden may clearly be interpreted as a metaphor for our early childhood days. We were born into the world and were provided loving homes, free from worries and concerns, where all our needs were provided for lovingly. We lived our lives as wonderful expres-

> Adam is told "Of every tree of the garden you may eat freely. But of the tree of the knowledge of good and evil you shall not eat, for on the day you eat of it you shall surely die" (*Book of Genesis* 2:16, 17). The verb in the Hebrew text is doubled to emphasized the certainty of the punishment for transgression, hence "surely die." So what does Adam do? As typically human, he eats of it. And then lives another 930 years (*Book of Genesis* 5:5).[25]
>
> — Gerald L. Schroeder, Ph.D.

sions of love. But soon our souls prodded us along our spiritual paths and introduced us to the experience of fear. And our fears cast us out of our children's Gardens of Eden, into the world to experience fear (*Book of Genesis* 3:22-24).

We then built our lives from this generated fear, and lived amid much pain and suffering. We are trapped by our own interpretations and false beliefs. We became slaves, captive to our lack of Self-love, just as the Jewish people were held captive as slaves by the Egyptian Pharaohs. Upon their release from this captivity, the Jewish people wandered for forty years in search of their Promised Land.

This seems like a pretty accurate, quite close, parallel description of my own life's "metaphor." When I was born, my two parents showered me with love and provided me with everything I needed to live comfortably. Then, as a young child, I gained my first experience of fear. I interpreted a particular event to mean "I wasn't lovable" and from then on generated my belief system based on a lack of Self-love.

Afterwards, I felt trapped, enslaved by this belief system. No matter what I did to attempt to break out and gain my freedom from these fears, it seemed as if I could never escape. I wandered through life in a barren desert of loneliness and frustration for almost thirty years, or until I was ready to move onto the next phase of my spiritual path.

In the Bible, the term "forty years" stands for "the length of time until completion."[26] It has been suggested that the reason the Bible's writers used forty years in this way was that forty years was the average life span in post-Egyptian Jewish times. Forty years therefore stands for a generation—not a literal forty years, but "however long it takes you to reach completion of a phase" of your spiritual journey. In my case, I wandered through my life, enslaved by my beliefs, until I was ready to complete this phase of my life and move on to the next step on my spiritual path.

Judeo-Christianity is certainly not alone in thus describing this portion of the human journey. We find a parallel story about the birth of ancient Buddhism—the story of Lord Buddha himself.

In 536 B.C.E., Lord Buddha began life as the child of Sākya King Kapilavatthu and his wife Queen Maya. Buddha's given birth name was Prince Siddartha. As Prince Siddartha grew up, King Kapilavatthu made sure his son stayed inside the palace, where Prince Siddartha was constantly surrounded and protected by the most elite guard of soldiers and given every possible comfort and luxury available in those days. So the prince grew into a man who had known only the softest pillows to lie on, the sweetest fruits to eat, the prettiest young handmaidens to wait on him, and the strongest guards to protect him. His handmaidens constantly wafted gentle breezes to keep him cool during the summer months and wove the finest silks and wool to keep him warm during winter. The prince grew up with no knowledge of misery, old age, sickness, poverty, or suffering. Doesn't that sounds quite similar to the Garden of Eden, just a few miles to the west and a few years later?

But when the prince reached the age of manhood, he became bored of living the same luxurious life every day. His heart grew with an intense desire to understand the world and explore what was beyond the palace walls. He ached for new experiences and a greater understanding of the real world.

After convincing his father to let him do so, Prince Siddartha left the palace on a carefully arranged tour of the city surrounding the palace. Before Siddartha embarked on his journey, King Kapilavatthu had ordered his army to remove the sick, impoverished, aged, and suffering people from the streets the prince was to tour. The army was further ordered to present a view of the city consistent to the inner palace environment.

But his father's prescribed tour did not satisfy the young prince, so he deviated from the planned route and went to explore forbidden parts of the city. There at last he saw another side of life. His eyes fell on the sick, the aged, and the poor, and his heart was filled with great compassion for all the world's suffering. In those moments he determined to dedicate his life to a journey to find the Truth, search for understanding of the real meaning of life, and find a way for all humankind to be released from its suffering and to live in eternal happiness.

> Thus Siddartha, the Prince, renounced power and worldly pleasures, gave up his kingdom, severed all ties, and went into homelessness.[27]

— *The Teachings of Buddha* 6.25

So Siddartha (no longer the prince) became a homeless man in search of Enlightenment. As his first task toward meeting this goal, Siddartha became a beggar and lived a life of impoverishment, going "from house to house silently waiting until someone offered him food."[28] Next, Siddartha lived for six years with five *bhikkhus* (religious zealots). During this time he practiced "severe austere self-discipline," living in severe deprivation and near-starvation. (This group practiced what was called "mortification," or the denial of all human physical needs.)

With the *bhikkhus*, Siddartha sat in silent meditation for days sometimes, without food and water, until the very verge of death. Then, after six years of this harsh suffering, Siddartha left the *bhikkhus* to seek Enlightenment on his own. After several more years of searching, Siddartha found Enlightenment and was transformed into the person we now know as Lord Buddha (which means the Enlightened One).

Under an olive tree during one of his periods of meditation, Siddartha experienced a revelation that led to his Enlightenment through what he called the Four Noble Truths. Summarized, these state that upon man's birth his inherent state is suffering, not achieving what he desires. Only through right understanding (of the Truth), right action (aligning his actions with the Truth), and right concentration (right thoughts) would man reach Enlightenment.

It was revealed to Buddha that the path of man's journey to Enlightenment is through an experience of pain and suffering. Man's inherent nature (as long as we live our lives based on fear-generated beliefs) is to experience suffering and frustration, and only through this experience can we reach Nirvana. (Nirvana means living a life without pain and suffering; it is not a place in time/space such as what many believe about Heaven.) Buddha's teaching tells us that we can transcend this pain and suffering, which he referred to as misery, once we gain a new and different perspective on life. We are doomed to experience misery as long as we continue to live in the ego, or from the foundation of fear-based beliefs. Only when we understand our Oneness with the Universe, when we align our consciousnesses and therefore our actions with our divine nature, can we overcome the fears that led us to our suffering. Once we have lived and understood our lives based on fear, we can then transform this experience into love (or Oneness with the Universe).

As I think you can easily see, the stories of Adam and Eve and Prince Siddartha parallel each other in almost every way. Both sets of characters began life in Gardens of Eden, places of absolute luxury where their every want was immediately satisfied. They knew nothing of pain, suffering, sickness, or strife. But just like Adam and Eve, Prince Siddartha took dramatic steps to seek out just these "fearful" experiences in the search for greater Enlightenment. They took dramatic actions that resulted in undergoing the experience of suffering, so they might really understand the experience of Eden (or Nirvana, in the Lord Buddha's case). Once they fully understood the experience of fear, and therefore suffering, they then were ready to discover their divine nature.

The Sufis say that this world can be heaven—when we love and bless one another, serve one another, and become the instruments for one another's inner growth and salvation. This world can also be a hell—in which we experience pain, betrayal, loss of love, and lack of caring.

Both aspects of the world are part of the divine order. This world is a place to taste the nectar of paradise and also to feel the coals of hell.[29]

— *The Essential Sufism*

Many of the great philosophers throughout history have also been teaching this concept that you must have the experience of suffering before you can fully experience joy for centuries. The late brilliant Lebanese poet and philosopher, Kahlil Gibran, described this concept in one of his most famous works, *The Prophet*:

Your joy is sorrow unmasked.

And the selfsame well from which your laughter rises was oftentimes filled with tears.

And how else can it be?

The deeper that sorrow carves into your being, the more joy you can contain.

Isn't the cup that holds the wine the very cup that was burned in the potter's oven?

And isn't the lute that soothes your spirit, the very wood that was hollowed with knives?

When you're joyous, look deep into your heart and soul and you shall find it's only that which has given you sorrow that's giving you joy.

When you're sorrowful look again in your heart, and you shall see that in truth you're weeping for that which has given you delight.

Some of you say, "Joy is greater than sorrow," and others say, "Nay, sorrow is greater."

But I say unto you, they're inseparable.[30]

**Joy exists because of sorrow. Pain exists because of happiness. The experience of love exists because of the experience of fear. Amazingly, in order for God to *experience* love, God needed to *experience* fear. God created this identity called "man" to live these experiences. God created man in His image, whose Divine nature was living in absolute joy, filled with joy, and true abundance and prosperity. Then God introduced the experience of fear, which is a step on the way to the opposite *experience* of our Divine nature. God devised this Divine Plan so we can truly experience our Divine nature—it is from our *experience* of our suffering that we can truly experience love.**

## We created lives based on fear, filled with suffering, in order to experience love.

When we experience this fear, we move from beings of love (young children without fears) into the second phase of life and the adoption of our beliefs that we are not lovable. The soul literally looks for any excuse it can use to adopt this belief system. We interpret our lives to generate the feelings and beliefs that we are not lovable, and this interpretation then causes us to create lives based on this interpretation. This fear invariably leads us to a life filled with pain and struggle. Yet through this experience of fear, we gain the possibility to fully experience a life filled with love and joy; only through the contrast of our not-love can we experience love. This is the divine gift that fear presents to us; in fact this is why nothing that God created is less than a perfect, absolute, divine gift.

As you probably are aware, **we live in a world of interpretations. The world happens around us, and our experiences of this world are based solely on our interpretations of it, which are in turn based on our beliefs and ideas.**

> Circumstance does not make the man; it reveals him to himself.[31]
>
> — James Allen

For example, remember Carmen's story from earlier in this book? Her fear was based on her interpretation that because her teacher embarrassed her she was not smart. Before her experience at the blackboard, Carmen was an intelligent, bright, shining, outgoing person; after those five minutes (seemingly a lifetime) at the blackboard, she adopted a belief that she was stupid and unlovable. Carmen became shy, introverted, risk adverse, and almost a recluse.

But think about it. Nothing really "happened" to Carmen during those five minutes; nothing in her life really changed. When those five minutes were done she was wearing the same clothes she had on before. She continued to live in the same house, she still had the same parents and siblings, and her friends still remained her friends. Even anatomically, she remained the same person after the experience that she was before. The only aspect of Carmen that truly altered was Carmen's interpretation of herself and the world. Had she adopted a different interpretation of that single event, her experience of that event and the rest of Carmen's life would have been very different. Her interpretation alone acted like a rudder in her life and steered her in the direction she took.

My experience was very different from Carmen's, but the *role* my interpretation played in my life was identical to her interpretation in her life. When my father sent me to my room, and then later scolded me for not informing him I was still there by the afternoon, I created the interpretation that I was unlovable. What happened to me was fairly inconsequential in the vast scheme of my life's experiences; yet my interpretation made this simple, terribly minor experience one of the most important of my life. My interpretation generated a belief system that I have based much of the rest of my life upon.

Again, **the soul looks for any excuse to adopt this belief system so that we will then experience fear. The soul will guide us to adopt an interpretation that will generate this lack of Self-love.** From this interpretation we then create a portion of our lives (for some of us it will be a major portion, for others it will be less) based on our fears. These fears will then generate lives filled with pain and suffering. And this entire process serves a higher purpose, a divine purpose.

As I'm sure you can see from many examples in your everyday life, the entire Universe operates on the basis of *duality*. Furthermore, **the Universe uses this duality to function as a kind of "spiritual biofeedback" device. When you align your Self with love, your life will be filled with joy and pleasure. When you align your Self with fear, your life will be filled with pain and struggle.**

The old analogy of the mouse in the maze and on the treadmill seems appropriate sometimes (in fact, many people call life a rat race). When the mouse finds his way to the desired location, he receives positive feedback; however, when the mouse runs the wrong way he receives negative feedback. (When he runs on the treadmill he gets neither, but he doesn't get anywhere, either.) The Universe operates in the same manner. The Universe provides us with both positive and negative feedback in direct relationship to our ability to live lives filled with love. This is our Higher Power's way of providing us instantaneous feedback on our progress towards living lives in which we become ongoing expressions of love (which is our divine purpose).

### And finally comes Enlightenment . . .

After these experiences, the cycle of our life continues and the next step on our paths is Enlightenment. A hairy caterpillar lives the first part of his life as a less-than-lovely creature, eating precious leaves in your garden. Yet he undergoes a tremendous transformation during his life. As a caterpillar he is dark and rather menacing-looking—not a creature you would normally gaze at to bathe in his beauty.

But the caterpillar then enters into a stage of metamorphosis; he is transformed from an unattractive creature to one of great beauty. As you complete this, the phase of your life that's filled with pain and struggle, *now is the time to begin your metamorphosis into the next stage of your life*—to learn to experience your Self-expressing love, and to have your life filled with experiences of joy and happiness. You are now ready to experience loving your Self.

Consider the experience of life as if you are attending school. You stay at one level until you learn all you need to learn at that level, and you can't begin the next grade until you do so. Only when you learn the lessons at one level will you be allowed to begin work at the next level.

**Each phase of life creates a foundation of experience and knowledge that's required for the next phase.** Your first phase of life was being born and living as a young child, expressing your Self openly and lovingly in all situations. Everyone reading this book has most certainly been born and had the experience of being an open and loving child. Your next phase was learning fear, and then creating a life based on your fears.

Lives based on fear invariably are lives filled with loneliness, pain, and suffering. I can assure all those of us who adopted deep-seated feelings of being unlovable that we have all learned this part of our life experience very well. I believe that anyone who has lived from this perspective for very long has experienced enough emotional pain to last a lifetime. So once you have been thoroughly indoctrinated in the pain and suffering of fear, you have the requisite experience and knowledge to move into the next phase of life. Now is the time to move to *Enlightenment*.

## It is now time to rebuild your life based on love, to experience joy and happiness.

Once you have successfully lived a life as a child, expressed love openly, and then experienced a life built upon fear, it's time to begin a life built on love. Your divine purpose on this planet is to experience yourself as love, and in doing so to experience God within you.

> Enlightenment is the natural condition that has no name after all the unnatural conditions that have names are stripped away.[32]
>
> — Ron Smothermon, M.D.

The fact that you are reading this book suggests that you already have a full enough knowledge of the experience of pain and suffering derived from living your life from fear. You are probably reading this book to help your Self find a way out of these experiences. Therefore, it is now time to fulfill your divine purpose. It is time for you to experience a life filled with the gentle knowledge of your worth as a human being, to experience a life filled with love and joy, to experience a life filled with a deep sense of peace of heart and peace of mind. How will you do this?

How is it possible for us to begin to experience lives of joy and happiness, when all we have known all our lives is struggle and pain? The first step in any transition toward Enlightenment is *to take responsibility for your participation in your life.* Enlightenment occurs the moment when we accept complete and total accountability and responsibility for our lives. Most of us with feelings of inadequacy have blamed these feelings on our parents or other family members, blamed the environment we grew up in, blamed someone else—sometimes anyone else—for our feelings and life experiences.

Now, blaming outside influences or being victims is neither wrong nor bad, it just will never get us what we really want in life. As long as we believe that someone else is to blame for the lives we're living, then we in fact must logically believe they alone have the power to change our lives. If they created them, then only they have the power to change them.

But if we instead take responsibility for our lives and if we understand that we actually created the lives we're living, then we alone have the power to change them. If we created the messes in our lives, then we have the power to re-create our lives into things our hearts really desire: lives filled with fun, joy, and love. (I'm not talking about taking responsibility so we can feel sorry for ourselves or beat ourselves up; that's just another victimization game, and if you play it, you will only continue to live more of the same life you have now.)

Like a child learning to walk for the first time, you have to take responsibility for falling down. Accept that falling down is only a part of the learning process, do so without judgment or comment, and be prepared to pick yourself back up, brush yourself off, and try again. Understand that you will make mistakes and accept them when you do; then learn from those mistakes, pick yourself up, and try again with your new knowledge.

---

**Enlightenment begins when we take responsibility for our lives. At that moment we also accept the power to re-create the lives we most desire.**

---

Take a moment and look back at your childhood and your life. Look at the decisions you made that brought you to the situation in which you're currently living. I ask that, instead of feeling upset, angry, hurt, or bad about your past decisions and behaviors, look at these in a new light.

Take a moment and appreciate these experiences in a new and fresh perspective. See the experiences of your life as integral steps in the Grand Design. See these experiences as laying the foundation on which you will create a new life built on feelings of confidence and fun. Take a moment and look at where you created interpretations that led to your lack of Self-love. Then look at where these beliefs have led you. And consider: Without these old experiences, you wouldn't have fully been able to experience and appreciate the joy of living a life filled with confidence and fun!

Take a moment and imagine what it would be like living a life filled with the gentle knowledge that you are a great person. Imagine the experience of living a life where you **KNOW** you're lovable. Imagine living the life you have always dreamed of. Then, once you have immersed yourself in your vision of your new life, look back at your previous experiences with gratitude, knowing that they were integral steps that laid the foundation for you to experience this new life. *You couldn't have gotten to the point of loving your Self without going through the pain; those previous experiences were integral parts of the foundation of your new life experiences.*

Look back and see if you can create a different interpretation of your life experiences that would help you today to generate Self-love where you once lacked it. **We can literally rewrite our childhoods by understanding our old interpretations and then choosing to adopt different interpretations of the same experiences.** If Carmen, for example, could have chosen to believe she momentarily froze at that blackboard, and that that event meant nothing that related to who she truly was as a person, then her definition of herself and her experiences would have been greatly altered.

> I saw a slogan on a t-shirt that said, "It is never too late to have a happy childhood." [33]
>
> — Bernie Siegel, M.D.

When I at last decided that my self-defining experience had no other meaning than that which I chose to assign it, I was literally freed from all those old interpretations and stories. Today, I choose to believe I'm a wonderful person who chose to seek a set of experiences that now allow me to deeply experience the love and joy in my life. To experience this richness now, I had to first experience the other side of that spectrum (which I most certainly have done). And you can choose to rewrite the story of *your* life just as easily.

**The only time we really consider making significant changes in our lives is when the pain of living our current lives becomes more than we can stand.** When we finally become overwhelmed with the pain and strug-

> The only person who welcomes change is a baby with a dirty diaper.
>
> — Anonymous

gle of our daily lives, when we finally are willing to admit that our best thoughts and ideas have only created lives that are not working, we are willing to consider change.

So this moment in our lives is crucial. We have built lives based on fear; we have experienced loneliness, shame, frustration, anger, and in many cases, desperation. And we have become deeply committed, emotionally, to these fears and made them the very foundation of our belief systems. We have created entire stories in which we most often play the victim and blame others. We have shared these stories far and wide; sometimes we have even hired therapists to listen to them after we bored our friends and families with them long enough. It's only when the pain associated with these beliefs and our stories becomes greater than our commitment to our flawed beliefs that we are willing to change.

I'll tell you candidly, at one time it took having my life almost completely collapse before I would be willing to admit that I had created a mess of things. My ego and my commitment to "being right" about how the world works and my whole dramatic story of my life were so great, it took an unbelievable amount of pain for me to break through that commitment. Once the pain became greater than my ability to stand it, only once the pain became greater than my commitment to those beliefs (including my story), *only* then was I willing to consider a different perspective. When that moment finally came, I was willing to do anything it took for the pain to be relieved—including taking responsibility for creating the painful life I was experiencing. But at that very moment, I began the phase of my journey called Enlightenment.

**Change occurs when the pain resulting from our beliefs becomes greater than our commitment to those beliefs.**

Once you do take responsibility and therefore claim the power to change your life, once you begin to look at even your past experiences in a positive light, then what do you do? The answer is quite simple: *Begin to live a life in which you express the greatest amount of love in every situation.*

To this point, because we have lived most of our lives through fear and built up our entire identities over-compensating for our feelings of being unlovable, it is not surprising that we probably don't know how to do this. For years, and perhaps decades, we have created and lived

(Jesus said),

*Verily I say unto you, Whosoever shall not receive the kingdom of God as a little child, he shall not enter therein.*

— *Gospel of Mark* 10:15

our lives from the habit of "being unlovable." Just as you would deal with any habit that no longer serves you, you choose to start a new *habit* today.

FIVE SECRETS TO SELF-LOVE

Jesus taught us the key to this new way of life when he said, "Receive the kingdom of God (all the joy and fun in life) *as a little child.*" Living as a child means living in a child-*like*, not a child*ish*, manner. Now, there is a significant difference between the two. I don't believe Jesus meant that we should be walking around throwing food at each other, or giving each other "wedgies," or forgetting all the good manners and lessons of our youth. No, Jesus was talking about beginning to live our lives *seeing the world in awe and as filled with miracles all around us.* Every day we should be noticing all the wonderful aspects of our lives; we should be taking the time and giving the attention to seeing the millions of miracles that are surrounding us every day. He was teaching us that we should feel free to express ourselves fully and completely as various emotions enter our hearts. He was teaching us to have the confidence to share our innermost thoughts and feelings with the world around us. We should feel confident and comfortable to laugh when we feel something is joyous or funny; we should feel strong enough to cry when we are sad or hurt.

When we were children, we didn't hold our emotions in for fear of what others might think, we openly shared ourselves. And among the wonderful things Jesus was teaching us to notice is that we our Selves are wonderful beings, just as we are today.

If we have spent several decades learning how to live our life based on beliefs and feelings of fear, after doing so for that long we have forgotten what it's like to live life any other way. So right here and now, I strongly invite you to keep in your imagination the image of a child learning to walk. The first step is wobbly and the child falls down. The second is a little steadier; then it gets wobbly, and the child falls down. The third step is stronger yet, and then finally the child is able to stand on his own two feet without wavering.

> It is the fear of the young bird to trust its wings. The experiences of the soul will fast out grow this alarm.[34]
> — Ralph Waldo Emerson

Then the child takes the next step, wobbles and falls down. This happens again and again, until finally the child can take two or three steps without falling. After each fall, the child jumps right back up and gets back to the task at hand. Sometimes we need to cry a little, and then attack a problem again. Once you have reached even one goal for the day, rest, enjoy, and feel good about your progress. Remember, each step you take is a victory, so celebrate *each* step in your mind.

Or keep in mind the image of a builder. Begin to build your inner confidence up one brick at a time, until your foundation begins to become solid. And remember this: Just because you may have spent thirty or forty or fifty years building and living your life from a place of fear and feelings of not being lovable, that doesn't mean it will take you that long to change. You can immediately begin to rebuild a foundation of Self-love, Self-respect, and Self-confidence *beginning immediately.*

Please allow yourself the opportunity to learn. Please allow yourself the opportunity to make mistakes. Please allow yourself the opportunity to grow into this new way of life—without kicking yourself every time you make a mistake. **The only people who don't make mistakes are those who don't do anything. You will make mistakes.** Accept that fact, yet love your Self for your efforts. After every mistake stand up and begin again, and celebrate each victory no matter how small. Soon you will begin to feel a new sense of inner strength and confidence. Soon you will begin to see yourself in a new light. Soon you will begin to relate to your Self and others through an entirely new perspective—as someone who is lovable just because you're you.

Here's some great news: *You* are in control of how quickly this transformation occurs. When you push down on the accelerator in your car, you send more gasoline into the pistons, propelling your automobile forward faster and faster. Just like you are in control of the speed of your car, you are in control of the speed at which you create your new life. The "accelerator pedal" in this transformation is your ability to be honest with yourself and your commitment to consistently apply the principles described in this book.

If you are willing to be absolutely honest with yourself, you'll know what or where you need to apply change in your life. If you are willing to concentrate and apply these principles consistently, then your habit of not treating your Self well will be transformed quickly. If you enter into this metamorphosis with absolute honesty and a solid commitment, you will see dramatic results quickly. You can begin to transform your life almost instantaneously, but it does require serious

The Sufis refer to a spiritual state as a "baby," because that baby is born in the heart and is reared and grows there. The heart, like a mother, gives birth, suckles, and rears the child of the heart. As worldly sciences are taught to children, the child of the heart is taught inner wisdom. As an ordinary child is not yet soiled with worldly sins, the child of the heart is pure, free from heedlessness, egotism, and doubt. The purity of a child appears often as physical beauty; in dreams, the purity of the heart's child appears in the shape of angels. We hope to enter Paradise as reward for good deeds, but gifts of Paradise come here through the hands of the child of the heart.[35]

— Sufi Sheikh Abdul Qadir al-Jalami

dedication and commitment. You will see results directly commensurate with your honesty and commitment. So let's begin to take that first step towards new life.

# Spiritual Truths Discussed in this Chapter

**As children, we are unlimited expressions of love.**

Children are unfettered expressions of their inherent love. As a young child, you felt safe to express yourself without restraints and without fears. You saw the world as a constant discovery of miracles in everyday life.

**Your divine purpose is to experience God.**

Every major religion teaches that your divine purpose on this planet is to experience God (or Spirit).

**God is love; God is the energy of love.**

Every major religion teaches that God is love. God isn't "loving," because that would imply God could be "un-loving." God is the very essence, the energy of love.

**We experience what we express.**

You can only experience emotions and feelings that you express. You can't experience another person's emotions towards you. You can only experience your own expression of your emotions.

**Your divine purpose is to become an expression of love.**

Because God is love, and your divine purpose is to experience God, then your divine purpose is to express your Self as love. Through expressing your Self as love, you will experience your personal divinity.

**The soul seeks a basis to generate a lack of Self-love, which serves the Higher Purpose of causing the soul to experience fear.**

When you were a young child, your soul searched and found an excuse to adopt a lack of Self-love. By doing so, your soul then experienced the pain and suffering this expression of fear naturally generated.

**We must experience fear in order to experience love.**

You must experience fear and the resulting pain and struggle this generates in order for you to experience love. The human mind requires contrasts for experience; you only experience love because and after you have experienced fear.

**We created lives based on fear, filled with suffering, in order to experience love.**

When you express your Self as fear, you generate your life filled with suffering and pain. Once you have experienced this pain, you are then ready to experience the depth and breadth of love.

**It's now time to rebuild your life based on love, and to experience joy and happiness.**

Because you have already experienced the pain and suffering from your fears, it's now time for you to experience a life filled with joy and love.

**Enlightenment begins when we take responsibility for our lives. At that moment we also accept the power to re-create the lives we most desire.**

When you accept responsibility and accountability for creating the life you are living, you then accept the power to create a new life filled with love. When you blame someone or something else for your life, you are refusing to accept the power to change it. Enlightenment occurs when you are willing to take responsibility for your life and claim the power to create the life your heart most desires.

**Change occurs when the pain resulting from our beliefs becomes greater than our commitment to those beliefs.**

You are only willing to change your beliefs when the pain resulting from these beliefs is greater than your commitment to being right.

# Part Two:

## Five Secrets to Loving Your Self

**W**hich is the great commandment in the law?

Jesus said unto him, *Thou shalt love the Lord thy God with
all thy heart, and with all thy soul,
and with all thy mind.*

*This is the first and great commandment.*

*And the second is like unto it,
Thou shalt love thy neighbour as thyself.*

– *Gospel of Matthew* 22:36-39

$A$ny path is only a path, and there is no affront, to oneself or to others, in dropping it if that is what your heart tells you . . . Look at every path closely and deliberately. Try it as many times as you think necessary. Then ask yourself, and yourself alone, one question . . . Does this path have a heart? If it does, the path is good; if it doesn't it is of no use.[1]

— Carlos Castaneda, *The Teachings of Don Juan*

## Chapter Three

# Pay Attention

The concept of developing a deep sense of Self-confidence and Self-love is simple—not easy, but simple. Before you begin each drive across the country in your car, it's usually a good idea for you to take a road map and plot your course. The first step in this process is to find out where you currently are "on the map."

"How do you get to Mt. Olympus?" a man once asked of Socrates. He replied "Just make sure every step you take goes in that direction." [2]

— Eric Butterworth

Imagine for a moment that your Self is a separate identity living inside your body. Let's take a moment and look at what your current set of behaviors is telling your Self. When you don't treat your Self with respect, and when you don't show love for your Self, you are telling your Self that it is not worthy of respect and it is not lovable.

When you act like you are not lovable, when you act in accord with what you believe at that moment is "right," then you send the message to your Self that you are not a "good" person. We've all heard the saying, "If someone tells you something often enough, eventually you'll begin to believe it." That's exactly what *has* happened and what *is* happening with your Self. When you tell your Self a million times a day that you are not lovable, then you believe it. After years and years of paying heed to this constant message, you will become thoroughly convinced. You adopt this belief as a fact, and you live your life based on this perspective.

Whenever you deny your true dreams and desires, you tell your Self that it doesn't deserve to have the best that life has to offer. When you blame others for your decisions, behaviors, and actions, you tell your Self that you aren't lovable if you aren't perfect, and that, because you'll never be perfect, you'll never be lovable.

When you feel you have something to say, but you don't say it, you tell your Self that you don't deserve to be heard. When you don't tell the truth,

> The underlying idea here is that ordinary people readily fear harm from others without giving equal consideration to how much they harm themselves.[3]
>
> — Thomas Cleary

you tell your Self that you wouldn't be lovable if the truth you don't tell were known. When someone compliments you and you deflect this compliment, you tell your Self that it is unworthy of recognition. Whenever you sabotage your Self, you again tell your Self that it doesn't deserve what's good. Whenever you become egomaniacal and brag about your Self, you tell your Self that the only way it's lovable is to convince those around you that you are something you aren't.

All these behaviors add up to you telling your Self that it is not worthy to be treated with respect—that it is not worthy of being recognized as good. You're telling your Self it is not worthy to be honored by telling its Truth. You're telling your Self it is not worthy to receive any of the good the Universe has to offer. So when your Self hears these messages enough times, it learns that it isn't lovable, it isn't worthy of enjoying the good.

As we have discovered, everyone on this planet has displayed this behavior at some time in his or her life. It's merely part of a spiritual path, part of expressing and therefore experiencing our fears. *Please don't beat your Self up when you begin to see and understand the nature and cause of some of your behaviors.* Instead, take this opportunity to be grateful that with the knowledge you now have you can transform your current experiences into experiences of Self-confidence and Self-love. You can now use this "inventory" to map your progress against, and you can quickly see tremendous progress if you are committed to making an honest effort.

To create a deep sense of Self-confidence and Self-love, you merely have to now treat your Self with love and respect. Also, you must act in alignment with your definition of integrity—begin living according to your definition of "right."

As we go through our daily lives, we have many opportunities to make choices, and as we meet these opportunities, we can either treat our Selves with respect and love or we can treat our Selves poorly. Your current habit, generated from the interpretation that you are not lovable, is to treat your Self with disrespect and no Self-love. We have built our entire lives based on these habits, these behaviors; now we have to learn new habits. These new habits will be a challenge for you at first; and then, as you integrate them regularly into your life, these new habits will become second nature. So your recipe to begin to experience a life filled with Self-love: Generate new habits, habits in which you treat your Self with love and respect.

When a painter stares at an empty canvas, he has in his mind a concept of the picture he wants to paint. He begins to color the canvas with broad strokes, brushing color in large swaths on the bare canvas. The painter applies the blue to the sky portion of the picture in wide, thick strokes. Once the painter has established the foundation of color, he then goes back with a fine brush and makes the clouds and the stars (say this is an early evening scene).

> Do not underestimate good, thinking it will not affect you. Dripping water can even fill a pitcher, drop by drop; one who is wise is filled with good, even if one accumulates it little by little.[4]
>
> — Gautama Buddha

As you apply to your life these new habits you've been learning about, you will see major improvement in your life almost immediately, just as the painter's broad strokes change the color of the canvas quickly. After you make the major changes, laying the foundation for your new habits, you will then spend the rest of your life fine-tuning these habits with increasingly finer and finer brushes and strokes. And you'll spend the rest of your life working on this process, in increasingly finer detail.

---

### Creating new habits of demonstrating love and respect for your Self will soon allow you to experience a sense of Self-love.

---

I would now like to share with you five "secrets" to help you develop new habits of treating your Self with respect and love. (Of course, once you read this book, they won't be so secret anymore—they're only secrets now because no one has taught them to you!) With this book, I intend to make these "secrets" well known. The five "secrets" to developing your new habit of treating your Self with love are:

**Pay attention**

**Take responsibility for your experience**

**Speak your truth**

**Keep your agreements**

**Ask for what you want**

Now, while each of these secrets may at first appear obvious and possibly simple in concept, it is not necessarily easy to learn each concept in depth and practice each one in your daily life. Most of us have spent years, if not decades, developing our old behaviors. It won't take you that much time to change your old habits, but it probably will take more than an afternoon's work to do so.

59

But I'm going to take each concept and explore it in enough depth so you can see how to apply them all in your life *immediately, today, without delay*. So, starting now, let's take these "secrets" or principles one at a time and work with one over each of the next five chapters. The first principle we'll talk about is learning to *Pay Attention*.

## Pay Attention

Maybe you've noticed: Most of us seem to wander through our lives on a sort of "automatic pilot." Yesterday we got up in the morning, ate breakfast, drove to work, worked until lunchtime, ate lunch, worked until it was time to go home, drove home, performed our evening routines, and then went to bed. Chances are, today we'll do the same and tomorrow the same.

But each day that we live the same lives, each day we do the same things, eventually we become numb to these routines. Let's face it: Most of us just don't think about what goes on inside our minds, and what behaviors we exhibit on a day-to-day basis. Most of us are living our lives like robots made of meat, not really thinking. We're just sleepwalking through our days, through our entire lives.

Many of us associate our senses of Self with our thoughts. **The first step to developing the new habit of loving your Self is to *become more fully aware of your thoughts*, your behaviors, and what is going on in your life.** Begin to *Pay Attention*—notice your thoughts without judgment, watch your thoughts move through your mind.

> There is something you do at the same time that you perceive something (create a mental picture with your imagination), you can't help it, because that's the way you're made as a mind being.[5]
>
> — Stretton Smith

Most of us believe in some way or other that we are our thoughts, dimly aware of them though we may be. But we are not our thoughts. Let's take a moment and conduct an experiment that will clearly demonstrate this. First, clear your mind. Now, whatever you do, don't think of a pink flamingo!

Darn it, you did, didn't you? A picture of a pink flamingo flashed into your mind; you had no choice about it. But my suggestion has made you aware of something about your thoughts. Before I suggested that you not think of a pink flamingo, I doubt highly that you *were* thinking of one. But when you made that thought in your mind—though it was my idea to put it there—you began to "own" it.

So it's important that you learn to watch your thoughts—see them objectively and understand those that will serve you and those that won't—to create the life you desire. As you begin to notice your thoughts, you will become more and more aware of a pattern in the way your mind assimilates and relates to information (data) received through your senses. Let's walk through a model of human thought processes, and I think you'll quickly understand what happens.

Your mind is in some respects almost mechanical in the way it processes information. As we humans grow and make our way through life, we develop experiences through many different circumstances and conditions. In each set of your circumstances, your mind catalogs the conditions and situation. It then catalogs the particular response that seems to work best for you in that situation, and saves these bits of information for future use. The memory for this data is located in the hypocampal memory system buried in the cerebral cortex of your brain.

Your senses collect information, then transmit the data to your brain through the nervous system and through the endocrine system. Yes, medical science has now determined that your body sends information to the brain and the body

> Sigmund Freud's theory of mind . . . The "reactive mind" . . . is an extremely stupid stimulus-response mechanism that is run by its memory bank: by mental "pictures" from the past, including "engrams" (deep peronsal traumas that become moments of consciousness or pain). According to this characterization, every time a person encounters a new experience which reminds him in any way of an earlier trauma, the reactive mind causes the individual to automatically act as he did before, in a stimulus-response fashion.[6]
>
> — Jane Self, Ph.D.

through neurotransmitters (e.g., endorphins, peptides, and other chemicals) as well as through the nervous system. Your brain then takes this input and searches your past experiences for anything that even vaguely resembles the current situation. The mind then finds the experience in your database that is closest to the current event. Once it has located a past situation that resembles the current situation, the brain then sends to your conscious mind the reaction you successfully used last time.

Scientists refer to this entire process in neurological terms as your Reticular Activating System. Generally you are not even aware this process is going on; it takes place billions of times each day, without your being aware of it. Let's go step-by-step and see how this works and how it impacts your daily life.

Let me give you an example of how this Reticular Activating System has worked in Mike's life. To make it clear, we are going to ask Mike to tell you something that happened very recently in his life. Let's listen now to Mike:

> *Just last month, I had an excellent lesson in how my mind works. My wife called me at work to talk for a few minutes. She proceeded to tell me how much she greatly appreciated the way I help her make sure the kids*

*are transported to and from their various sporting events. (Our children are all involved in different sports and have different practice and game times at different parks spread throughout the neighborhood.) Christine also went out of her way to tell me that she'd noticed I've been making an effort to help her around the house more and that she appreciated all my efforts. She went on to thank me for all this, and for being thoughtful enough to stop and pick up dinner one night when both of us were running around doing our family taxi service.*

*But towards the end of our conversation, which lasted about ten minutes, Christine told me she would also appreciate it if I made more of an effort take the garbage cans out to the street before I go to bed on Thursday evening. (The trash service comes very early Friday morning, and sometimes if I wait until Friday morning I miss it; when this happens, we can't empty the trash cans in the house for the week, because our outside containers are generally full.)*

The lower serf is like a thief who sneaks into your house at night to steal whatever is valuable and worthwhile. You cannot fight this thief directly, because it will mirror whatever force you bring against it. If you have a gun, the thief will also have a gun. If you have a knife, the thief will have a knife as well. To struggle with the thief is to invite disaster. So, what can you do?

The only practical solution is to turn on the light. The thief, who is a coward at heart, will then run out. How do we turn on the light? Through the practice of remembrance, awareness, and heedfulness.[7]

— Sufi Sheikh Tosun Bayrak

*Well, when she brought up the garbage, I immediately felt hurt and I "shut down." I stopped talking. Even when I came home that evening, I didn't say more than three words all evening long. I got up early the next morning and went to work, once again without saying a thing to my wife or kids. That night, I stayed at work late, 'till almost eleven. I carried this pattern on for several more days, until finally my wife cornered me and made me talk to her. I realized that this was a pattern that occurred regularly in our lives and has always left me feeling lonely and my wife angry.*

*Now, I committed myself to breaking this pattern, and I began to dissect what was really happening below the surface in my thoughts. Let me take you through what I discovered, step-by-step.*

*My wife had called me at work, and we had a very pleasant conversation. She complimented me several times on me making a concerted effort at helping her around the house. She must have said "Thank you" and "I really appreciate you" at least a dozen times. Then she made one little constructive suggestion—and all I heard was "Mike, you aren't doing enough around the house! You aren't smart enough to know that the garbage cans need to be put out the night before. Boy, are you so dumb I have to tell you when to take the trash out?"*

*Notice in particular: Although my wife complimented me a dozen times and gave me only one small gentle reminder,* **all I heard was negative, harsh criticism.** *She could have said a thousand wonderful things about me, but the only thing I would hear was the one thing that I could possibly interpret as negative. And I realized that my habit whenever I perceived any criticism whatsoever was to shut down, stop talking, and withdraw from everyone. Sometimes I could hide out for days, even weeks, to avoid any possible contact that might lead to more criticism.*

*Thinking about it, I came to see that every time I heard criticism it reminded me of my dad telling me that I was stupid and that I'd never amount to anything. I'd hated him for that; in fact, I'm still very angry at him today for making my life miserable. My life and how I deal with things today are all screwed up, and it's all my dad's fault. Whenever someone says anything that I might construe as telling me that I'm not smart, that I'm no good, that I'll never be successful, I hear my father's voice yelling those very words to me when I was a child.*

*But when I began learning that these are just my learned, stored responses to criticism, I began to see a different way to look at these thoughts. Let me explain. First, I now know that whenever someone says anything to me that might remotely sound negative, my mind searches its database for "deposits" of criticism I've heard before. It finds one in my memory that resembles what I've heard today, and then sends that same response to my brain. Even though someone may be speaking very positively to me, one little comment that might possibly be interpreted as negative can threaten to ruin all the positive feedback. If it does, then I do what I did as a child—I go and hide. When my father would yell at me, I'd go to my room or find a place in the house to go and hide; and I'd avoid him for the rest of the day, sometimes even the rest of the week. If he couldn't find me, if he didn't see me, I thought, then he wouldn't yell at me.*

*But when I learned that's how my mind works—that I interpret today's adult conversations through my childhood experiences—I saw clearly that I was reacting to my wife today just as I reacted to my father when I was only five. So I've been acting like a five-year-old my entire life, because that is what I learned was "successful" back then.*

*Well, for years that behavior has robbed me of having any kind of intimate relationship with my family. But I now have learned to Pay Attention, look at my original reaction, to think about whether or not that reaction is a good one for today. Now I can decide how I want to react as an adult. My reactions aren't just automatic anymore; I can retrain my mind to react according to what it takes to show my wife I love her; I can react in a more loving and understanding way, rather than just hiding from everyone.*

Thank you, Mike! We greatly appreciate your sharing your deep personal thoughts and feelings with us.

Now, something like what happened to Mike happens to all of us millions of times a day. When Mike was a child, an event occurred about which he created an interpretation that told him that he was unlovable. The event in his situation involved his father's acting out his anger and alcoholism. When Mike's father told him that Mike was stupid, when he yelled at Mike that he would never amount to anything, Mike interpreted these remarks as telling him that he was unlovable. Mike's interpretation was certainly understandable. When this event happened, Mike learned to run and hide from his father to protect himself from this kind of verbal assault.

> While forming such a judgment seems to be a lightning-fast reaction, it does take place in real time. And it does not happen automatically: there is a distinct process that makes such reactions possible, a process called attention.[8]
>
> — Mihaly Csikszentmihalyi, Ph.D.

From then on, Mike interpreted anything anyone said through a mental "filter": "Can this be construed as negative criticism?" If it could possibly be interpreted in this manner, Mike considered whatever this person said as an attack, and his brain sent the response he learned as a child to protect himself: withdraw—run away and hide. But while this response served Mike as a child to avoid some verbal abuse from his father, this "survival" mechanism doesn't serve him today.

Yes, Mike's programmed survival response may have "worked" when he was a child, but in his life today that same programming results in creating a life filled with loneliness and isolation. Mike has an incredibly loving wife and a great family that cherishes him and loves him; yet his reactions learned when he

> . . . [T]here are no circumstances capable of invalidating you. Only you are powerful enough in your life to invalidate you.[9]
>
> — Ron Smothermon, M.D.

was a five-year-old child ruin his life and his relationship with his wife today. The old survival reaction, "run for your life," was programmed into his brain some thirty-five years ago. Yet in the incident Mike has just shared, even though his wife gave him ten great compliments, told him how much she loved him, and thanked him for all his thoughtfulness, he couldn't hear any of that. As soon as she said anything that even remotely resembled criticism, his brain forgot all the positives and only focused on the negative. His pre-programmed response, learned when he was a five year old, kicked in, and Mike concentrated only on his childhood negative interpretation.

As a result, Mike lost out on the experience of hearing his wife tell him that she loved him and appreciated all his thoughtful gestures. Mike turned a loving, thankful conversation into one filled with accusations and attacks—all because of the response he'd learned as a five-year-old child protecting himself from his father.

Once Mike began to see what was happening in his life, once he understood that he was reacting and living his life from the perspective of a five-year-old child, once he saw the destructive nature of his behavior, then Mike had begun to **Pay Attention** to his thoughts and reactions. Now, Mike still feels the same *initial* reactions as before to this kind of situation. But by Paying Attention to these situations, Mike now has the ability to *decide* if those reactions will serve him to create a loving, intimate relationship with his wife and family.

Once Mike begins to Pay Attention, he notices his thoughts, and then he begins to choose thoughts and behaviors that create a life filled with romance and intimacy—and he allows himself to be vulnerable. As Mike acts to make different choices today, he begins to retrain his mind. In a fairly short while, Mike's mind will move from his former, immediate reaction of "running and hiding" whenever he's faced with either confrontation or criticism, to the new reaction of being able to stand in the midst of the situation and seek the most favorable outcome for Mike.

Pay Attention. Watch your thoughts. As you notice your reactions, stop and take a split-second and ask your Self, "Does this reaction serve me well, or is it merely some pre-programmed response from my past?" When you're in the midst of a situation and you see your "old habits" and behaviors happening, just stop and ask your Self, "What can I do that will demonstrate the greatest amount of love for my Self in this situation?"

When you aren't demonstrating love, you can be assured the Universe will send you a subtle (or sometimes not-so-subtle) message letting you know you aren't. **When you aren't expressing love, you'll generate life experiences filled with pain and struggle.** Pay Attention to your thoughts and reactions. Watch your thoughts. Retrain your mind. Don't automatically accept your brain's first reactions. Consider the implications of those reactions. Then consciously choose the reactions, thoughts, and behaviors that will serve to generate the life you most desire.

> The TRUTH is that when you become conscious of the fact that your mind is serving up survival pictures from the past—and then you choose to take a hard look at those pictures—the effects of them immediately diminish. And if you continue to look them squarely in the eye—to "tell it like it is"—the effects will disappear completely. Because you will then realize that you have a choice to make: whether or not to let your pictures of similar situation run your life.[10]
>
> — Carl Frederick

65

The negative reactions you have today were generally all learned and recorded within your brain between ages 2 and 8. And as you start noticing more and more of your thoughts, you will soon find that many of these childhood-based reactions and the resulting behaviors don't serve you to create the life you most desire.

A caution: As you begin to understand the cost of your behaviors to your life, you may start to feel angry at the thought of the many years you've lost living your adult life based on reactions and behaviors you learned in childhood. *Don't allow your Self to sink into this thought process.* Don't begin to feel bad about your Self because you didn't understand this dynamic sooner. Most people on this planet never become aware of how their minds work. And until you were ready to hear, until you were ready to see, nobody could have told you about this in a way that you would have heard and seen.

Sure, you probably heard many of the bits of wisdom you will find in this book at some time or other; but you never really were able to put them into a context that made much sense or made a real difference in your life. That's because you just weren't ready; you had not learned what you needed to learn at your current level, and you just weren't ready to take the next step up. You could only become aware of this higher-level thinking when you had learned enough, you had experienced enough, and you had built a solid-enough foundation to support this higher level of thought and living.

**Paying Attention allows you to monitor your thoughts. Paying Attention allows you to choose which thoughts will serve you to live a life filled with Self-love.**

You know, life is so amazing: During the very time I was writing this section, I had still another learning experience in Paying Attention. Although I've been practicing the principles of Self-love I'm teaching you for almost ten years now, I still have moments when the old programming pops up. Yesterday my wife informed me she'd found signs that mice had been in our den. We live out in the country, and each fall and winter the mice come indoors looking for food. I've been tasked with the responsibility of catching these mice and removing them from our home. (Yes, if you're an animal rights person reading this, I do use humane traps—catch 'em alive and then I feed them to my pet python named Monty.)

Learning to pay attention is perhaps the most basic part of personal growth. The *Attentive Awareness* of which we are now speaking is not a casual state of mind. When we refer to *paying attention* as a Point of Power, we mean *paying attention 100%*. When you pay attention *completely*, life is transformed.[11]

— Peggy Dylan Burkan and Tolly Burkan

Anyway, the moment Cheryl told me about the mice I instantly felt myself becoming defensive. I stopped, noticed my immediate reaction, told myself she wasn't being critical, she was just letting me know what she'd found. I then thanked her for the information and set some traps in the den.

My old programming was that anyone saying anything that might possibly be interpreted as criticism would immediately get me defensive and upset, and I would feel criticized and unlovable. I know now that this reaction doesn't serve me, so when I noticed it popping up, I then chose a different interpretation and went on the business of loving my wife without interruption or upset. This is what I meant earlier by "fine-tuning"; it's also an excellent example of Paying Attention.

For your encouragement, let me say this: The continual practice of Paying Attention to your thoughts, your actions, and your behaviors will present you with many gifts throughout your life. Virtually every time I've made a silly mistake that cost me either a little money or time I've made it as a result of not Paying Attention. And many of these experiences left me feeling pretty dumb. As an excellent example of this lesson, let me share with you something that happened to me a couple of months ago.

I was driving to Outback Steakhouse® when a man in a huge SUV acted like he owned the entire road. Well, I allowed myself to react to his rude driving style instead of just ignoring him. When we both drove into the restaurant's parking lot, as I was pulling into the first available parking spot, I glared at the driver as he passed by. I jumped out of my Jeep, intending to further demonstrate my displeasure at his rudeness. Boy, was I going to glare at him—that would show him (like he really cared what I thought)!

But just as I got out of the Jeep, I pressed the "lock" button on the door—without grabbing my keys from the ignition—and slammed the door. I locked my keys in the car while I was busy thinking angrily about that rude driver. So intent was I on the thoughtless behaviors of someone else, I neglected to Pay Attention to what I was doing. The result was that I had to call a taxicab, wait almost thirty minutes for the cab to show up, pay $45 for a ride home, and then waste another twenty-five minutes while someone drove me back to the parking lot to pick up my Jeep.

I wasn't paying attention to my initial programming, to my behavior; I was reacting to someone else's rudeness, and it cost me almost two hours of my life and $45 in cab fares. I didn't Pay Attention, and I ended up feeling pretty dumb because I hadn't done so. Having acted so silly made me feel dumb again, only reinforcing my old, childish programming. I needed instead to Pay Attention to my reaction, and to remember that I'm not that old programming. But once I got over my initial reaction and my silly behavior, I thought, *The Universe is so wonderful; it has so many different subtle ways to demonstrate the lessons we need to learn!*

Here's another story I'll tell on myself. About a year ago, I was driving home late one evening, and I decided to stop by Wendy's® for a quick dinner. ( Yes, sometimes I do cook and eat at home.)

I yelled my order into the speaker on the stand and was told the price. The person inside then told me to drive to the first window, which I promptly did.

Just as I was handing over my money, I got a cell phone call I'd been waiting for. The Wendy's employee inside handed me my change and asked me to pull forward to the next window. But I got so engrossed in the phone conversation that I just pulled out of the parking lot and drove off towards home. When I was about ten minutes away from home, I finished my phone call—and only then did I realize that I hadn't pulled up to the second window to pick up the meal I'd already paid for!

Well, because it was late and I was tired, I just completed my drive home, feeling pretty dumb about my silly mistake. Now, looking back at this experience and many others in my life, I realized that very often when I failed to Pay Attention, I made silly mistakes that not only cost me money, time, and inconvenience, but often also left me feeling rather dumb.

By Paying Attention, we eliminate many of these silly mistakes that make us feel dumb about our Selves. And that's just one good reason why the first step towards learning new habits and experiencing life in a different manner is to Pay Attention. Learn to watch your thoughts. All too many times we live our lives without even thinking, and when we live that way we make silly mistakes that make us feel dumb and sometimes can reinforce our already low Self-esteem. Today, when I make a silly mistake, I just remind myself I'm human. I stop and laugh at my silliness and then let it go. I don't dwell on it. I don't allow it to make me feel bad about my Self.

Before we begin learning to Pay Attention, we also tend to allow thoughts to enter our head without considering what kind of process is happening—without taking account of how these thoughts have built habits that have caused us to lack Self-respect and Self-love. But as you become aware of your thoughts, you can ask your Self, "Does this thought serve me?" If it doesn't, you merely let it pass through your mind without comment or judgment. Then you can ask your Self, "What serves me the most in this situation that will be my greatest expression of love?"

Paying Attention allows you to watch your life with the sense of awareness necessary to shift your experiences from fear to love. Paying Attention allows you to generate new habits, new behaviors, that will soon begin reinforcing your love for your Self.

## In order to . . .

Lack of Self-confidence and Self-love generate behaviors that validate those very same old beliefs that have caused us fear and misery. We create vicious cycles that sometimes feel impossible to escape. When we feel negative about ourselves, we act negatively towards ourselves, which in turn brings us negative feedback. We have just read several different examples of just this kind of behavior. We have also seen that we can retrain our minds by creating habits and behaviors that continually reinforce to us that we really are lovable and worthy beings.

To retrain our minds this way, we must Pay Attention to our thoughts and behaviors. When we find ourselves having thoughts lacking in Self-love, or when we see ourselves displaying behavior that springs from lack of Self-love, then we have to stop and replace those thoughts or behaviors with positive reinforcement.

**Whenever we do anything "in order to" gain approval or love, we're telling our Selves we aren't lovable for who we are.**

One of the strongest tests of our thoughts is to watch for thoughts and behaviors that show up *"in order to . . ."* These thoughts and behaviors are the results of those old thought patterns originating from a lack of Self-love. Anytime you do anything "in order to," you act out of fear. Anytime you do anything "in order to," you tell your Self you are not lovable the way you are; you need to pretend to be some other way to be loved. But this kind of pretending doesn't work, either. When you do anything "in order to" sound smart, your audience only walks away with

> One of the most difficult lessons to learn for ambitious young people is that when you try to make an impression, that is the impression you make.[12]
>
> — Eric Butterworth

the feeling that you are trying to seem to be smart. When you do something nice "in order to" be perceived as being nice, your audience only sees you trying to *seem* to be nice.

You see, when we say something "in order to" seem smart, we're telling our Selves we are not smart enough to be loved the way we are, that we need to be viewed by our audiences as "very smart" "in order to" be respected and loved. We're telling our Selves that we are not lovable because of who we are and what we are now. Furthermore, when we attempt to sound intelligent, we're telling our audiences that we are trying to look smart. That's the impression they're going to have: *This person is trying to look smart.* Just as we ourselves shake our heads at other people we know are working too hard to look smart, so does our audience whenever we attempt to make ourselves look intelligent.

The same holds true when we put forth efforts "in order to" look pretty, in order to appear loving, in order to appear to be nice, or in order to make an impression. Whenever we display this kind of behavior, we're telling our Selves that we aren't worthy or lovable the way we are, that we need to be seen some different way in order for people to love us. So this behavior ends up merely degrading our already fragile Self-images. Furthermore, our audience usually can sense that we aren't being genuine. They can immediately sense we're overcompensating for our feeling unlovable, and they'll adopt less-than-positive impressions of us. So all this behavior does is let our audiences know our terrible secret, the one we wish to hide the most.

Paying Attention allows you to ask your Self, am I doing this or saying this "in order to . . .?" If the answer is "yes" or even "maybe," then remind your Self you don't need to do this to be lovable. Usually, it's best to just be quiet and allow the conversation or situation to take its natural course without interjecting your two cents. Sometimes it's comforting to allow other people to do the talking, and to listen instead of feeling like you have to participate and make a favorable impression. Pay Attention to what you're doing, Pay Attention to why you are doing this, and then decide to act only when you are not doing something "in order to . . ."

Again: Stop, take a look at your behavior, and ask yourself, "Does this behavior serve me?" Occasionally, the answer may be "yes." Because I felt so unlovable as a child (due to my belief that I wasn't smart enough), I developed a great memory. With this talent, I could impress those around me with all sorts of facts, trivia, and bits of information. I did this "in order to" make myself appear smart enough to be lovable.

Now, while the behavior of attempting to impress others with my memory "in order to" gain approval doesn't serve me, my fine memory itself does. I've developed this strong, positive talent (at first cultivated for the wrong reason) in ways that now serve me well. When I lead workshops, I can share a great deal of information without the aid of notes. I can keep my attention on my audience without burying my nose behind a podium or sheaf of paper.

So please don't throw your baby out with the bathwater. If you become aware of doing a certain behavior, first seek the good in it. If you find out that the behavior doesn't serve you to demonstrate respect and love for your Self, then make the choice to change that behavior. If you find behaviors that do serve you, feel grateful. Pay Attention to your thoughts and actions and appreciate your strengths.

At this point, I would like to introduce you to Melinda. Like Mike, Melinda has lived a life filled with insecurities and lack of Self-love. Mike's and Melinda's backgrounds are very different; Melinda's family members didn't have alcoholism to deal with, but they displayed their own brand of human negativity. Melinda shares:

> *I was the youngest child of a large family. I had two older brothers and three older sisters. My family was generally very loving and generous, and although we were never rich when I was young, we never wanted*

*for the basic necessities. My family was also loving and giving towards even our extended family; for instance, we took in several of my cousins when their families couldn't take care of them.*

*But even though my family had this loving, generous side, they also had another side (as most families seem to).*

*For some reason unknown to me, I became the butt of many family jokes. I was constantly told that I'd been adopted, after having been left on the front doorstep one evening by gypsies. I was told that I was the "white sheep" of the family, since my family was of non-white ethnicity. I knew that this jibe was only my family's way of showing their affection and demonstrating their sense of humor. Yet after years of hearing this "kidding," deep down inside I began to believe some of it. In fact, I began to believe that I was really not part of the family; I felt like an outsider, like I was never loved and accepted as a "real" family member.*

*Many times when I was young I felt like I was being picked on, and that wasn't the type of attention I wanted. One day, I make a silly remark and everyone in the room laughed and noticed me, seemingly in a positive way. Then I made another joke and I heard someone say, "Wow, she's pretty funny!" Since that moment on, I began to work to make up more jokes so I could become more the center of attention.*

*This has continued into my adulthood, though I now work as a consultant with one of the major consulting firms on the East Coast. I've always been the first person in every room to tell a joke. I've always been that person in each crowd who tries to become the center of attention. Whenever I go out with my friends, I'm always "the life of the party." Whenever a topic of conversation gets too intense or intimate, I make a joke and steer things to a "safer" topic.*

*In rare moments of honesty and reflection, I will admit—but only to myself—that this behavior leaves me feeling rather empty and void of any real intimacy in my life. I'm just so afraid that anyone who really knows me won't like me or they won't love me, so I don't let anyone get anywhere near close. I can see that this behavior tells my Self that the real me is not worthy, not lovable, and so I've had to create distractions so no one can really see who the real me is.*

*But as I have begun to Pay Attention and have been watching my behaviors and thoughts, I've noticed that whenever I feel inadequate, whenever I feel like everyone is smarter than I am, I either try to make a joke or otherwise draw attention towards myself. The other day I was in an important meeting with several members of a new-client company that had just hired our firm. I was intent on making a good impression, and after listening to the client's president explain his business and what help he wanted our firm to provide, I saw myself rushing into the conversation to crack a joke. It was almost like I was outside my body, just like watching a movie, watching myself make this joke. I knew I was doing it at the most inappropriate time in the meeting, and that I was making a joke in order to draw the attention to myself so as somehow to gain the client's approval.*

*Well, I made an impression, all right, but not one I wanted to make. Watching the client's and my co-workers' faces, I saw their eyes roll, and could read that look. I could tell I'd made just the opposite impression from what I'd intended. Thankfully, I caught myself almost doing the same thing several more times in that meeting, but those times I kept quiet. From then on I only spoke when I had something important to add to the meeting.*

*As I continue to watch myself more and more, I catch myself doing this stuff more and more. Each time I've caught myself wanting to say something in order to make a good impression, I remind myself I do not need to do that. I remind myself that the quality of my work says everything that needs to be said.*

*After about a month of meeting with that new client, several of their people and several of my co-workers and I all went out to lunch to celebrate the success of a project we'd all cooperatively worked on. As we were walking from the car to the restaurant, my client's president quietly confided in me that his team had been rather concerned about me after our first meeting; it had seemed like I was one of those people who had nothing to offer, aside from being a jokester. After that first meeting they thought I'd spend all my energy and time being the disruptive class clown. He told me he was very glad he'd been wrong about me, and that first impressions aren't always correct.*

*Not only did that help boost my confidence, I've noticed that I've started to feel stronger and more confident around other people, knowing they're appreciating me for just me instead of for some façade I've been putting on. In the past, whenever someone did acknowledge me for anything, I always had to wonder if he or she really appreciated the person I am or the act that I had been putting on. Now that I've been working to not put on my act, now that I've been just myself more and more, I'm getting a lot more praise and appreciation from people. And it feels wonderful.*

Notice that Melinda realized that she was making jokes and disrupting conversations "in order to" draw attention to herself. But by truly Paying Attention, she was able to watch her thoughts. She thought about why she was joking and discovered she was exhibiting this behavior "in order to" draw attention to herself because she didn't feel she would get that attention just because she was Melinda.

Melinda also saw that her efforts actually were having the opposite effect—people were not taking her seriously because she wouldn't allow them to. Once she saw that this behavior was actually having the opposite effect from the one she intended, she began to make the conscious choice to avoid making jokes at inappropriate times. Melinda is still a very funny person, but she's chosen to share that side of her personality only when it's appropriate, not when it would demean her efforts to be regarded as a competent professional.

**Many of us exhibit such behaviors "in order to" get attention, to prove our worth, or to overcompensate because we don't feel lovable.** Some of these behaviors serve us well in the world, some don't. *Pay Attention.* When you find that certain behaviors don't serve you, make a conscious choice to change those behaviors. Know that you're a great person, just because of who you are. You have nothing to prove to anyone. You're already wonderful, just the way you are.

## Take care of your Self

**One of the fastest ways to begin to generate a sense of Self-confidence and Self-love is to begin to take care of your Self.** We all have several areas in our lives in which we know we should be taking care of ourselves, but for some reason or another, we aren't. When we don't do those things we know we should, when we don't take care of our Selves, we're just practicing still more ways of telling our Selves we aren't worthy of the effort.

What I've learned is that in several areas in our lives we can always make a quick difference.

We can begin to demonstrate the habit of loving our Selves, and we can quickly begin to feel the results. The examples below may or may not apply to you specifically; but I believe you will be able to identify areas in your life where these concepts apply. Some of the more typical of these areas are:

*Medical issues you are not tending to (high blood pressure, diabetes, etc.).* Make an appointment to visit the appropriate medical professional (whether a medical doctor or a practitioner of alternative medicine, if that's your choice). Then follow the professional's instructions (such as completing any procedures necessary or taking any prescriptions that are ordered).

*If you haven't done so recently, visit your dentist and begin to follow an appropriate oral hygiene regimen.* Whatever issues you have here, tendto them in a timely manner also (getting fillings, having root canal, etc.).

*Begin a responsible exercise plan and start eating more appropriately, if necessary.* Please be kind to your Self—don't use this as another excuse to commit to something and then not follow through, and then feel bad about your Self. See your doctor (or an appropriate health professional); develop a reasonable plan that begins slowly and gently builds; and be responsible in applying the recommended program—and follow through with it.

*Begin to responsibly handle your financial situation.* If you don't already have a budget, sit down and set up one. Your budget should out-line how you will be able to live within your means. Figure it so that, once you pay off all your bills, you can begin putting at least a little money in savings each month. Save as much as you can while still living comfortably. Then begin to exercise the discipline needed to stay within your budget. At the end of each month, when you begin to look at your statements and see your debts diminishing, see your savings increasing, and see that you are living financially responsibly, you will begin to feel good about your Self.

*If you're in debt and have been avoiding your creditors, call them and acknowledge your debt to them.* Then tell them you are committed to paying them every dollar you owe them and are working to create a plan to pay all your creditors in full. Next, ask them if they can work with you on payment plans with lower interest rates that would lower your monthly payments. All they can say is "no," and if they do, you are no worse off than you are right now. Regardless of how they respond, begin to make the minimum monthly payments even if it means taking another job (or finding a job that pays you more money) or lowering your current standard of living until every creditor is paid in full.

*If your home is cluttered or not clean, then create some time on your calendar and clean it up.* Clean out those old closets, either throwing away what you don't use regularly or donating the excess items to charity. As much as possible, clear out your living space so that it's neat, tidy, and uncluttered. Living in clutter, living in a space that is not clean, is just another way of not honoring your Self. You deserve to live in a neat, tidy, clean space. You deserve to live in a space you're proud of, not one to which you are ashamed to bring your friends and family.

*As you go through life, whenever someone compliments you, don't deflect or reject the compliment.* Just accept it with humility and grace. Simply answer, "Thank you." When you don't accept a compliment, once again, you're telling your Self you aren't worthy of the compliment. So accept the compliment, bask in the glow of those good feelings for a moment, and then let 'em go and get on with life.

One of the fastest ways to begin to build a sense of Self-worth is to begin to take care of all these kinds of "little things" you already know about in your life. Taking care of your body, taking care of your financial responsibilities, and taking care of your living space are all integral parts of honoring your Self. Take one area and work on it until you have completed your task. Sit back for a moment, celebrate your achievement, treat your Self to a reward, and than tackle the next area. Soon you'll have your life back in order, and you will begin to build a strong sense of Self-confidence. Pay Attention to how you're treating your Self. *Love your Self.*

## Taking care of your Self demonstrates Self-love and Self-respect.

Let's hear from Melinda in this area:

*About five years ago I went to a dentist, and he discovered I had a cavity. I paid him to fill it for me. The entire process was very painful, and since then I've avoided going back. I do brush regularly and occasionally floss my teeth, but for some reason I've not seen a dentist for the past five years. And it got to the point where I felt too embarrassed to even go into a dentist's office because I didn't want to hear him lecture me on not going more regularly. I felt embarrassed because I know we all should visit the dentist at least twice a year and have our teeth cleaned and taken care of. I felt ashamed and embarrassed that I'd let this go on for so long.*

*But part of my commitment to take care of myself, to treat my Self with love, was to take care of my Self medically. So I made an appointment and went to see a different dentist. I told him I knew I should have gotten dental care more often, but I hadn't heard and didn't want to hear a lecture about that. He understood and just went about the business of checking out my teeth. He found and filled one small cavity. The whole process was relatively painless, and now I feel much better about myself, knowing that I'm now taking better care of me.*

*In another area of my life, I realized that I'd been avoiding one of my creditors. I owed several hundred dollars to a department store for a purchase I'd made there about three years ago but just never paid them. Whenever I received a letter from their credit collection agency, I felt ashamed and embarrassed; I immediately threw their letters away, often without even opening them. It was like I was trying to escape this unpleasantness in my life—out of sight, out of mind. Yet that shame was always right there under the surface. I knew this situation was hurting my credit; I knew I couldn't get another charge card as long as this issue went unresolved.*

*So I finally got up the nerve and called the department store and asked to talk to the credit manager. I explained to her that I owed the store money, and I was looking to make the situation right. We talked for a while, and she seemed understanding, and said she was willing to work with me to create a payment plan my budget could handle. The manager even offered to help me out by reducing the amount of interest I owed. Within about thirty minutes, I was able to transform a situation that caused me grief and embarrassment to one in which I'm starting to feel good about my Self. Today that bill is paid off completely. It felt great when I wrote out that last check. I felt like I had part of my Self-esteem back again.*

*I've since taken a close look at my life and begun to do all the little things I've been needing to do to take care of my life. By taking care of the little things, by taking care of my basic responsibilities, I've also begun to feel like I'm finally taking care of my Self.*

## Listen to your Self

Once you begin the habit of Paying Attention to your mind, also begin to Pay Attention to your body. **Your body will provide an excellent guide to how you are treating your Self. When you're doing the things you know you should for your Self, then your body will feel good. When you aren't taking care of your Self, then your body will feel tense and will tell you so.** Whenever you do anything that disrespects and doesn't honor your Self, your body naturally reacts, giving you a sign that you aren't in alignment with your divine nature.

When you exhibit behavior that doesn't demonstrate love for your Self, your body releases chemicals into the bloodstream. These chemicals transmit information within your body, causing your body chemistry to change in reaction to the events you are experiencing. For example, when you are either upset or scared, your body releases peptides, causing your blood pressure to rise, your heart rate to increase, and a heightened sense of awareness. These are the body's natural reaction to fear, part of its self-survival mechanism. While short-term exposure to these effects does not harm the body, long-term exposure to these chemicals becomes toxic. If you continue this behavior long enough, then your body becomes overwhelmed and loses its ability to flush these toxins out of your system. Eventually these toxins have negative long-term health implications.

> . . . [H]appiness is our natural state, that bliss is hardwired. Only when our systems get blocked, shut down, and disarrayed do we experience the mood disorders that add up to unhappiness in the extreme.[13]
>
> — Candace B. Pert, Ph.D.

The system that seems to be the most susceptible to these toxins is your immune system. If you subject your immune system to enough of these toxins over an extended period of time, you can seriously damage your immune system's ability to fight disease. Diseases that are associated with this damage include, but aren't limited to, cancer, leukemia, diabetes, arthritis, and obesity.

Whenever you exhibit behavior that's disrespectful to your Self, your body will tell you. Your soul and your Self are aware of these behaviors, even when your conscious mind is not. You may have noticed that when you're acting out of fear, you often hold your breath and you temporarily stop breathing. Many times you also break out into a sweat. Pay Attention to your body and listen to your Self. You will begin to notice when you're acting out of fear. You will easily see what is happening with you, and you will begin to notice and make choices about your behavior.

Correspondingly, as you begin to take care of your Self, your body will react accordingly and give you feedback to this positive behavior. Your body will release endorphins into the bloodstream. Endorphins are chemicals within the body that act as information transmitters. These endorphins enter into the bloodstream and then move towards the brain, where they interact with receptors within the cerebral cortex. Endorphins are called the body's natural opiates because they attach themselves to the receptors in the brain and induce wonderful feelings of bliss. Endorphins actually stimulate your immune system, making it stronger. From this, you become healthier and you begin to feel wonderful.

Listen to your body, watch your body's reactions, and learn to interpret these reactions. Paying Attention to your body can help you find out where you aren't taking care of your Self and find out how to re-create new habits that will lead to feeling wonderful and becoming healthier. Listen to the feedback the Universe and your body are giving you regarding your thoughts, beliefs, and behaviors related to loving your Self.

Your body sometimes acts at a higher plane than does your consciousness. **The body can sense when you aren't taking care of your Self. The body acts like a report card telling us how you're doing in this respect.** Listen to your body, notice what's happening, notice how you're reacting to different situations. Your body will give you invaluable feedback—it's a great tool once you are in tune with its reactions.

Pay Attention to your body, learn to listen to its reactions, and you'll see with greater clarity where you're loving your Self and where you are not. When you find an area in which you aren't demonstrating love for your Self, don't beat your Self up; instead be grateful for the information— you've now found one more area you can easily transform from frustration and pain into love and joy.

## Living in the moment

An ancient story is told about a young man who was studying to be a rabbi, but was a major worrier. He always fretted about what might happen if this or that calamity occurred, or if not worrying about the future, he'd worry about something that had happened in the past. In other words, this man was a tangled mess of worries, causing him much frustration in his life. He couldn't concentrate on his daily studies or tasks.

One evening, the headmaster of this worrywart's rabbinical school called him to his office and suggested that he spend some time with one of the most learned of his Torah Professors. The young man was excited about the prospect of studying with one of the great religious teachers of his time. But when the headmaster suggested that the young student stay only one month with the Torah Professor, the prospective rabbi was puzzled. He asked the headmaster, "How can I learn everything I need to know about the Torah in only a month?"

The headmaster gently and patiently said, "Young man, I don't want you to study the Torah with the Professor; I want you to study how he ties his shoes."

Naturally, the student was confused. But, you see, the headmaster wasn't really telling the rabbinical student that he wanted the student literally to learn how to tie his shoelaces; he was suggesting that the student learn *how to live each moment* **in the moment.**

The headmaster knew that the Torah Professor lived in the present moment and was totally involved in each moment's task at hand before shifting his attention to his next task. Because the Professor concentrated on each task in the moment, he was able to take each simple task he performed throughout the day and complete it excellently. Because he focused his entire concentration on each task, he wasn't distracted by any worries or concerns. Because he fully concentrated in the moment, because he completed each task he performed with excellence, at the end of the day he could sit back and enjoy a day filled with many accomplishments. He finished each day filled with the satisfaction that his day was filled with excellence, and he slept well each night with a peaceful heart and mind.

You can perform a simple exercise each day that will allow you to begin to sense what the Torah Professor lived. Take twenty minutes each day and live them "through your fingertips." As you perform one particular task, such as washing the dishes at night, concentrate fully on the sensations and feelings in your fingertips. Become fully aware of each sensation, each feeling, each pressure point: the temperature of the water, the silky texture of the dirty water, etc.

Spend that entire twenty minutes completely concentrating on the sensations reaching your fingertips. Clean each dish, each glass, each utensil thoroughly and excellently, concentrating on your fingertips' sensations. Or, if you can't think of some task for your hands, then take a twenty-minute walk each day and concentrate on the sensations and feelings of the bottom of your feet.

When you are engaged in performing these tasks, your concentration completely focused, you won't be thinking about the past or the future. You won't be worrying about anything, you'll just be living for that moment. Most people find that within just a couple of days they have some quite profound experiences

> Ideas generate currents, as a fire under a boiler generates steam. The idea is the most important factor in every act and must be given first place in our attention if we would bring about any results of a permanent character.[14]
>
> — Charles Fillmore

while doing this sort of exercise. (If you don't, don't worry; keep working at it and just enjoy the break from your worries.)

**Why worry about the past? It's come and gone, and there is nothing you can do to change it. Why worry about the future? It isn't here yet, and your worrying generally won't change it anyway. No, all worrying does is make you miserable in the present.** *The only time that does exist is here, now, the present moment.* Why make your Self miserable now worrying about something you can't change or forecast?

So, don't. Stop worrying. When you find your Self worrying, remind your Self to be grateful and happy now, and then find something that distracts your Self. Do something that makes you feel good about your Self now.

I confess that chocolate ice cream usually works well for me. Sometimes I pick up a book that I find soothing or inspirational. Sometimes I watch a "feel-good" movie or I play with my two beautiful dogs. One sure way to make your Self feel good and stop worrying about your situation is to give of your Self in helping someone less fortunate. Volunteer your time at a local shelter, volunteer to visit patients in the local hospital, or reach out and help a family member

> Gratitude comes from the Latin *gratus*, which means pleasing, and *itude*, which means a quality or state of mind. So literally, *gratitude* means an attitude of pleasure. *"It is your Father's good pleasure to give you the kingdom."* [*Gospel of Luke* 12:32][15]
>
> — Eric Butterworth

or friend who has a problem. By giving of your Self in a non-selfish manner, you'll feel good about your Self, and you will no longer have the time or energy to worry.

The present moment is indeed the Universe's present to us (no pun intended). That's why we're talking about living in the present tense, because it's a present. Don't waste that present on useless energy and worry. Take each moment as a precious gift (or a present from our Higher Power). Invest your energies in making each moment the greatest you can imagine. Pay full Attention to the current moment, and you will be rewarded.

> But giving thanks in advance is the multiplier of your good. The fast and best multiplier of good is giving thanks—feeling grateful—before the arrival of the good.[16]
>
> — Stretton Smith

## Living in gratitude

One last and final technique of learning to Pay Attention: Begin to keep and maintain a Gratitude Journal. Every evening before your shut off the light to go to sleep, write down at least five new events, feelings, thoughts, activities, and so on that you feel grateful for having in your life. Make sure each item in your journal is unique, one you have not written down before. Find at least five unique things to be thankful for each day. Write each item down in as much detail as you can remember. Take several moments between each item and just sit in gratitude, thanking your Higher Power for the gift of this item. (Make sure you take a moment the next day to try to thank any person involved in this item.)

Then when the new day begins, as you go through your daily activities, make a mental note (or write down in a notebook) new items to be grateful for as you become aware of them. As you find each new item for which to be grateful, take a moment and express your gratitude silently to your Self. If any of these new items involve another person, take the time as soon as you can to express your gratitude to that person: "Thank you for giving me the raise in pay, boss; I appreciate your acknowledgment of my efforts at work." Or, "Thank you for helping me fix this credit problem; I know I will sleep a lot better now knowing this is behind me."

In the evening, take a few minutes and write down at least five new, unique items for which you are grateful. Then take a moment after you write each one down to thank your Higher Power and just to sit in the moment, filled with gratitude.

## Keeping a Gratitude Journal will direct you to concentrate on the positive aspects of each day.

You will find the first week of this exercise fairly easy. We all can name twenty or thirty things we're grateful for. After a week to ten days, however, you will run out of easy-to-find items for which to be grateful. Then you'll have to begin to Pay close Attention to find five new unique items each day. But you will find you won't have time to worry about the nonproductive stuff; instead, you'll be focused on the wonderful events, places, people, and things that flow into your life.

Then, some time in the second week, you'll run out of the simple things to be grateful for, and you'll be required to spend more and more of your energy seeking out new and unique miracles to be grateful for. And you won't have the time or energy to worry about the past or the future. Instead, you'll have to spend your mental energy recognizing all the miracles that exist in your daily life. And you'll soon **become "as a child," expressing your gratitude as you feel the emotions and seeing the miracles in your everyday life. Paying Attention will allow you to see as a child each new gift, each miracle that currently exists or happens in your life.**

# Spiritual Truths Discussed in this Chapter

**Creating a new habit of demonstrating love and respect for your Self will soon allow you to experience a sense of Self-love.**

You have created habits of not demonstrating Self-love and Self-respect over the years. So begin to create new habits that are active demonstrations of Self-love and Self-respect. Soon you'll begin to feel the difference—you'll have a deepening sense of Self-confidence and Self-love.

**Paying Attention allows you to monitor your thoughts. Paying Attention allows you to choose which thoughts serve you to live a life filled with Self-love.**

Over the years, you have generated behaviors that continually send the message to your Self that you are not lovable. Paying Attention to your behaviors and thoughts allows you to identify these and to proactively make choices to change. By Paying Attention, you can change your behaviors and thoughts to build up your sense of Self-love.

**Whenever you do anything "in order to" gain approval or love, you are telling your Self that you are not lovable for who you are.**

When you feel inadequate, you often try to overcompensate for these feelings. When you display behaviors "in order to" gain someone else's acceptance, approval, or admiration, you're sending the message to your Self that you aren't lovable just the way you are. Instead, you are telling your Self that you need to be more than you are "in order to" be loved. Remember that you are great, just the way you are. Pay Attention to these behaviors, and make conscious choices as to whether or not your behaviors serve you to express Self-love.

**Taking care of your Self demonstrates Self-love and Self-respect.**

By taking care of your Self, you are actively demonstrating Self-love. Taking care of your life is another way to quickly develop a deeper sense of Self-love and Self-respect.

**Keeping a Gratitude Journal will direct you to concentrate on the positive aspects of each day.**

Keeping a Gratitude Journal is a technique to begin to shift your daily focus towards recognizing the many miracles that exist in your life instead of worrying about what people think of you. Each evening write down in a notebook five unique things you are grateful for. Soon you'll be seeing new miracles in your life, wherever you look.

$\mathbf{F}$ailure is an opportunity.

If you blame someone else,

there is no end to the blame.[1]

*— Tao Te Ching*, Chapter 79

## Chapter Four

# Take Responsibility for Your Experience

### Don't judge your Self

Our divine purpose is to experience our Selves as love (or the energy of God). In order to do so we must also experience our Selves as not-love (or have the experience of our Selves expressing fear, anger, hatred, jealousy, etc.). **We must experience the pain and struggle of living lives from a consciousness of fear in order to build the foundations to truly experience love.**

(Jesus said)

*Our Father does not judge us—we do that on his behalf!*[2]

**To accomplish this, God created us to make mistakes.** God created us in a way that ensures that we naturally experience fear beliefs that then generate lives filled with pain and struggle. So when we find ourselves doing this, we shouldn't judge ourselves, because we are only doing what we were created to do. There is no right, there is no good, there is no wrong, there is no bad. There is only that which causes us pain and suffering and that which causes us love and joy. There is no value in judging your Self. Judging your Self only keeps you mired in negativity and pain.

So, as you begin to Pay Attention and Take Responsibility for Your Experience, please don't beat your Self up for having experienced a life filled with fear. If you feel you need to be "punished" for your beliefs, then please consider the current pain and suffering in your life as more than adequate "punishment."

Consider the analogy of life as a classroom, where you have to spend time in one grade so you can build a foundation for the next level. You can't begin working on subtraction before you learn how to perform addition. If it takes you longer to learn addition than someone else, there is no right or wrong, there just is.

You are not a "bad" person just because it takes you nine months to learn addition, even if other people can learn it in less time. Your brain just takes a little longer to understand this particular concept. You are not a "better" person because you can learn addition in only six months. Either way, you aren't worse or better, you're just who you are.

If you take nine months instead of the "average" eight months to learn, you merely must stay and work on your addition until you thoroughly understand its principles before you may begin to learn subtraction. But in this case, the "addition" class isn't very much fun, and the "subtraction" class is highly enjoyable (unlike my recollection of those math classes in school).

**There is no right, there is no wrong, there is only that which serves you to create the life you most desire, or that which doesn't.**

As you begin to Pay Attention to your thoughts and your actions, you will begin to see more and more fear-based beliefs and actions. You will also begin to notice more and more of your unlikable behavior. You will notice more and more of the kind of your behavior that's out of alignment with loving your Self. Because you're reading this material, I'm sure you've already experienced enough pain and anguish in your life, and you're ready to change these painful beliefs and behaviors to others that will bring you more love into your life. As you become aware of negative thoughts, beliefs, and behaviors, you'll be faced with two choices: Are you going to take responsibility for them—or are you going to blame someone else for them?

> If you create an experience in your life which you view as pleasant or worthy, you will be most willing to be responsible for it. You may even be "proud" that you did it, which is a step away from responsibility. However, when you create an experience in your life which you judge as bad or unpleasant, your mind will have the tendency to disown the authorship of the experience.[3]
>
> — Ron Smothermon, M.D.

## Take Responsibility

A young woman went to her mother and complained about her life and how things were so difficult. She talked at length about all the abuse she had suffered as a young girl at the hands of her alcoholic father. Although he had passed away almost ten years ago, the daughter still blamed her father for the fact that her life was filled with struggle and misery. She said she did not know how she was going to make it in life and wanted to give up. She was tired of fighting and struggling; it seemed that as soon as one problem was solved a new one arose.

After her mother listened to her complaints, she silently took the girl to the kitchen. She filled three pots with water. In the first, she placed carrots; in the second, she placed eggs; and in the last, she placed ground coffee beans. The mother let them sit and boil without saying a word. In about twenty minutes she turned off the burners. She fished the carrots out and placed them in a bowl. She pulled the eggs out and put them in a bowl. Then she ladled the coffee out and poured it into a bowl.

> Man is made or unmade by himself; in the armory of his thought he forges the weapons by which he destroys himself; he also fashions the tools with which he builds for himself the heavenly mansions of joy and strength and peace.[4]
>
> — James Allen

Turning to her daughter, she said, "Tell me what you see."

"Carrots, eggs, and coffee," the daughter replied. The mother brought her closer and asked her to feel the carrots. She did and noted that they got soft. She then asked the daughter to take an egg and break it. After pulling off the shell, the girl observed the hard-boiled egg. Finally, the mother asked her to sip the coffee. The daughter smiled as she tasted its rich flavor.

The daughter then asked, "What's the point, mother?"

Her mother explained that each of these objects had faced the same adversity—boiling water—but each reacted differently. The carrot went in strong, hard, and unrelenting. However, after being subjected to the boiling water, it softened and became weak. The egg had been fragile, its thin outer shell protecting its liquid interior. But, after sitting through the boiling water, its inside became hardened. The ground coffee beans were unique, however. After they were in the boiling water they had changed the water for the better.

"Which are you?" the mother asked her daughter. "When adversity knocks on your door, how do you respond? Are you a carrot, an egg, or a coffee bean?"

Life happens. People do things; people do things to us and they do things around us. Sometimes they do things that directly affect us. Most of the time, they do things that don't directly affect us. Sometimes things happen that we have no control over. **Not a single spiritual or religious teaching has ever stated that "life is fair." Life isn't fair—but it isn't unfair either. Life just is, life happens.**

You're NOT responsible for anyone else's actions. You're NOT responsible for what happens *around* you. You're NOT responsible for what happens *to* you in many instances (especially when you were a child and incapable of protecting yourself). **You're NOT responsible for anything over which you have no direct control. You are, however, 100 percent responsible for what you choose to do about whatever happened or didn't happen to you. How you choose to live your life is your choice, and you're responsible for your choices.** How you choose to react is your choice, and accordingly, you're responsible for your choices.

This may sound harsh, even cold, but it's one of the great lessons you need to learn. It really doesn't matter what happens or who did what to whom. *The only thing that matters is what you choose to do about whatever happens or didn't happen.*

People do things. Some people engage in inappropriate actions and behaviors. You're NOT responsible for anyone else's actions. People do things around you. Some people act out in fearful, destructive ways in your presence. You're NOT responsible for what happens or what these people do around you.

Some people prey on the helpless, young, or disabled. Some people participate in highly inappropriate behavior with people who aren't capable of protecting themselves. You're NOT responsible for what happens *to you* in many instances (except if you're an adult who's capable of protecting himself or herself). Life happens.

But life certainly didn't seem very fair to my friend Wanda, who was born with genetic physical birth defects. She isn't responsible for the condition of her body when she was born. She is, however, absolutely responsible for what she chooses to do about her condition. She's 100 percent responsible for her reactions, her interpretations of her condition, and what type of life she chooses to live. She can choose to live her life filled with anger and resentment, or she can choose to live her life looking for opportunities to be joyous and to see the Love in all situations. Either choice is fine; one choice is just more fun than the other choice.

Carmen, from the *Oprah* show, wasn't responsible for her teacher making her stand up at the blackboard for five minutes because Carmen couldn't remember how to work the math problem. Mike wasn't responsible for his father's alcoholism or the abuse he encountered as a child. Francesca wasn't responsible for the behavior of her schoolmates. None of these people were or are responsible for the behaviors and actions of anyone else.

Yet each of these people is completely responsible for their reactions to what happened to them and for the choices they've made and will make regarding how they live their lives in response to these events. Each one of them can choose to live his or her life from feelings of anger and resentment, blaming others and acting the victim. Or each one of them can choose to seek the lessons in his or her situation, learn what is available to be learned from them, and choose to live happy and healthy lives filled with joy and love.

Again, you are NOT responsible for the behaviors and actions of other people. You are not responsible for anything in your life over which you don't have complete control. You are, though, responsible and account-able for your *interpretations* of the events and circumstances of your life. **You are responsible for all the choices you have made and are making and the manner in which you're choosing to live your life. You can make the choice to blame others, or even your Self. You can make the choice to not blame anyone, and instead seek the good from the situation. You can choose to live a life filled with anger, or you can choose to live a life filled with joy. Either way,** *it's completely your choice.*

Now, while you're 100 percent, completely responsible for the interpre-tations you made as a child, please don't beat your Self up for having made those choices. Beating your Self up doesn't change your life. Once you understand what's happening, make a different choice. Choose to find the lesson, the good, in the experience. Then choose a new inter-pretation that empowers you to create the life your heart most desires.

If you choose to blame someone or something else, or blame your environment for the status of your life, you're not accepting accountability and responsibility for your thoughts, your beliefs, and your behaviors. If you make this "blaming" choice, then you're really deciding not to change.

If you choose to believe that anyone other than you is responsible for your thoughts or behaviors, then you're choosing to believe that the other person, and he or she alone, has the power to change your life. If you're saying, for example, that your parents caused you to have your neg-

> Being a victim justifies any-thing the mind cares to act out, no matter how destructive to yourself or others.[5]
>
> — Ron Smothermon, M.D.

ative beliefs, or that they're causing you to behave in a certain way today, then they alone hold the power to change what they caused. If you're telling your Self and the world that you're insecure because of something your parents did to you many years ago, then you're also telling everyone that only they have the power to un-do that particular event. (Logically, if they had the power to create your thoughts, your beliefs and your behav-ior, then only they have the power to change them.) I call this kind of blame-casting "playing the part of the victim."

Playing the part of the victim is what happens whenever you blame some-one or something other than your Self for your thoughts or beliefs. Playing the victim means you refuse to accept as yours the power to change your life. And this constitutes a decision on your part to not change—a decision to continue to live the same life you have been living and are living today, a decision to not risk the change required for you to live a greater life.

I invite you right now to strongly consider whether or not living the same life you're currently experiencing will ever put you in a position to experience life filled with Self-love and joy. While the decision to blame others isn't a "wrong" decision, it just may not serve you in your journey to a life filled with Self-love.

## Playing the role of the victim means you're refusing to claim the power to change your life.

You can also exercise another choice—to ignore the situation completely. But in that case you're also making a decision to continue living your life the same way you are today. Because you are reading this book, you probably aren't happy with your current way of living, and you're looking to make a change. Just be aware that ignoring the situation, living in denial, choosing not to make any decision is making a decision to continue to live the same life you're living today.

> Being responsible is a spiritual characteristic. It takes seriously the insight that the Rain-God (Spirit) has made us with the gift of being able to make choices. And we're making choices all the time. Even the decision to do nothing is a choice that we're making. The choice NOT to make a choice is still a choice.[6]
>
> — Father Leo Booth

If you make that decision, you'll only continue to experience the pain and struggle that currently fills your life. This is also not a "wrong" choice; it just will probably not allow you to live a life filled with Self-love and will prevent you from experiencing your divine nature.

If, on the other hand, you choose to accept accountability and responsibility for your thoughts, beliefs, and behaviors, you'll be accepting the power to make the changes that will allow you to live a life filled with Self-love. **By taking responsibility and accepting the fact that you are solely responsible for your experiences and your interpretations, you'll also be accepting the power to change those interpretations.** As I mentioned earlier, according to my definition, Enlightenment begins when you take complete responsibility for your experiences. When you take that responsibility, then you claim the power you've always had to make the changes necessary to begin to live a life filled with expressions of love.

I have a close friend who seems to have repeatedly chosen "wrong" dating partners. She's inevitably found someone who eventually betrayed her trust and broke her heart. While she was in the midst of her last grieving process, she asked me, "Grant, why do I always seem to make the wrong decisions about

> The fact you have problems in life does not make you a victim, but handling your problems from the position of victim does.[7]
>
> — Ron Smothermon, M.D.

men?" I in turn asked her, "What do you gain by making these wrong decisions in terms of your dating partners?" She said she didn't know.

We talked about it for a while, exploring what may or may not have been happening. In the end, she saw that she was deathly afraid of being vulnerable and of putting herself fully into a relationship. Deep inside, she felt that if she chose an emotionally healthy partner, and she put herself fully into a healthy relationship and then it didn't work out, she wouldn't know whom to blame. Instead, if she makes poor choices in her partners and the relationships fail, she can always blame her poor choices.

With this attitude, she was destined to always have poor relationships. She would avoid taking the risk and therefore also attempt to avoid responsibility for trying to have a great relationship. But ultimately she would always pay the price and continue to have one failed relationship after another.

> **Taking responsibility for your experiences gives you the power to change your life towards experiencing Self-love.**

Here's one of the more interesting perspectives in this area: **Whether or not we believe we're taking responsibility for our lives, there is no way we can avoid doing so. You are responsible—whether or not you accept the responsibility. Your beliefs and your behaviors directly dictate the experiences you have in your life. Your choices will directly dictate the life you experience.**

When you live from love and joy, your experiences will reflect such. When you live from fear, your life will be filled with pain and suffering. No one else is living your life; no one else has to live the consequences of your beliefs and behaviors. You're going to live the consequences, so you might as well accept the power to decide what they will be. You and I might pretend to not take responsibility, but in the end, we will all have to take the ultimate responsibility.

> **You can't avoid responsibility for your life; whatever your beliefs and behaviors are will dictate how you experience your life.**

Let's let Mike share another story, this time regarding his own revelation about taking responsibility.

*A little earlier I told you my father was an alcoholic. He was very abusive towards his children, and most of the time I seemed to be the primary target of his anger. Whenever he screamed, yelled, and/or hit me, I would run away from him. I sometimes hid out and avoided him for days after one of his tirades. This was my "successful" way as a child of dealing with his temper. Through this, I learned to avoid any and all confrontations. When I became an adult, I continued to handle all confrontations the same way.*

*I also took away from these early experiences the interpretation that whenever anyone said anything to me that wasn't 100 percent complimentary, I heard that comment as harsh, destructive criticism. Whenever my wife tried to talk to me about anything she wanted me to do, I could only hear my father yelling at me, telling me what a miserable person I was. This led me to want to go and hide, and I avoided my wife and kids for days, sometimes weeks, at a time.*

*As a result, all my personal and work relationships were a total mess. I didn't feel close to anyone; I felt lonely deep down inside for years and years. For decades, I hated my father for doing this to me. Finally, I saw that blaming him was in fact robbing me of my ability to change. As long as I kept carrying the perspective that my father caused me to be this way, then I was saying that only he had the opportunity to change me.*

*While attending a workshop to overcome my anger, I heard the story of identical twins who grew up in the same family, yet became entirely different types of personalities. One twin was loving and generous; the other was filled with rage and meanness. The lesson being shared at the workshop was that it isn't our environment or even what happens to us that charts our lives, it's only the interpretation we carry around that's important.*

*It isn't what happens, it's what you do about it. When I took a long, hard look at my situation, I immediately recognized that my father was a man who experienced tremendous pain. He didn't know how to handle this pain, so he drank. When he drank he shared his pain in mostly inappropriate ways, like yelling and hitting. His anger and pain had nothing to do with me; it was no reflection on who I was as a person; I just was the target of his anger at that moment. I wasn't responsible for my father's alcoholism or his abusive behavior.*

*Whenever my dad either hit or was yelling at me, I created the interpretation that I was unlovable. To a young child, this certainly seemed like a valid interpretation. As an adult, I can now see that another equally valid interpretation is that my father was a man in tremendous pain, and the way my father expressed that pain was abusive, and his abuse was primarily aimed towards me. His expression of his pain and fears had nothing to do with the person I was. He was just expressing his pain and suffering in an inappropriate manner that had me as its object.*

*Changing my interpretation doesn't mean the abuse didn't happen. Deciding to view hurtful actions in a different light doesn't in any way change what happened, or whether or not my father's behavior was appropriate. His actions were unhealthy, and they were inappropriate at best. Choosing a different, more empowering interpretation only changes what I'm going to do about the experience. I can choose a different interpretation, and in doing so, I can literally change my experience of the situation.*

*I also recognized that I've been blaming my father all these years for my hiding from others and myself. I realized that I had become the victim, refusing to take responsibility for my life. It had seemed easier to be miserable, blaming my father for ruining my life. For some reason, that seemed to give me some satisfaction. Yet in the end, I alone became miserable, lonely, and unhappy. My playing the victim left me powerless to create an even mediocre life, much less a great one.*

*Today, my immediate first reaction still is to avoid all confrontations, to run and hide whenever I hear anything that's too personal or that sounds like criticism. But I now can see this reaction coming, and when I recognize it, I take a deep breath and choose to react different-ly. Instead of closing down and hiding, I now choose to talk to the other person. I find out what he's really trying to tell me, and then I try to figure out the best action so we both get what we want. It doesn't always work, but it seems to the vast majority of the time.*

*This approach allows me to communicate, to avoid hiding, to make connections with people and keep them. My wife, my family, and I've begun to really get to know each other for the first time in our lives. It's amazing how wonderful it feels when you begin to experience genuine closeness with those you love.*

I observed that a close personal friend of mine, Kathy (not her real name), seemed to express a great deal of anger and resentment whenever she mentioned anything even remotely associated with her ex-husband. One day I shared my observation with her, and she readily admitted that she was still very angry with him, even though they've been divorced for many years.

Out of my love for Kathy, I explained to her the many health risks related to carrying around anger and unresolved bitterness. According to some of the latest findings in medical science, among the primary causes of obesity, arthritis, leukemia, diabetes, and cancer are unresolved anger and bitterness. I told her of a study done in California within the last several years that concluded that the root cause of most of the diseases of the immune system was unresolved negative emotions. I expressed my

> Health is not just a matter of thinking "happy thoughts." Sometimes the biggest impetus to healing can come from jump-starting the immune system with a burst of long-sup-pressed anger. How and where it's expressed is up to (you) ... The key is to express it and let it go, so that it doesn't fester, or build, or escalate out of control.[8]
>
> — Candace B. Pert, Ph.D.

concern for her health and welfare and gently asked if she had considered releasing the anger she'd derived from this situation. She said she had tried, but didn't know how.

I asked her to explain to me what had happened that caused her so much pain and anguish that she was still angry after so many years. Kathy explained that she was carrying around her anger against her ex-husband because he was "such a hateful jerk." She'd given him chance after chance, and he'd continually let her down. Each time he betrayed her trust, she felt more and more hurt. Each time he let Kathy down and cheated on her, she felt more and more invalidated and became more and more angry. He repeatedly fooled around on her, he lied, he cheated, and he always seemed to let himself get caught. It seems that she always caught him, almost as if he *wanted* to get caught. Yet she said she forgave him many times and kept giving him additional chances.

I listened to Kathy tell her story for many minutes, until she finished. Then I told Kathy that I was sure her story was absolutely accurate and truthful—from her perspective. I'm sure that what she said was only the tip of the iceberg, and she certainly seemed to have many reasons to be angry. I then also gently asked her if she understood that her story left her being the victim and with no power in the situation, and I asked if she thought that was really what had happened. I also asked her who she was *really* angry with: him or herself?

She looked at me, and clearly stunned, almost said something to me and then stopped. Kathy thought several minutes, and then a light seemed to come on in her eyes. She said strongly and boldly, "I wasn't the victim."

She told me she could have and probably should have left her husband after the first time she caught him being unfaithful. She was really angry with herself for having given him so many chances to hurt her. She also realized during our conversation that she realized her ex-husband had really been trying to get out of the relationship by using affairs and then purposely getting caught. But each time this happened she wouldn't let him out—even though he really wanted out. Kathy later talked to him, and he confirmed that this had been true. He told her that he was miserable in their relationship and actually never tried to hide his affairs from her. He thought each time that she would catch him, she would break up with him, and he would be free.

We talked about what lessons and what good had come from their relationship. We talked about the many blessings he had (if inadvertently) shared with her through this entire experience. Through this relationship, Kathy had begun to realize her own Self-worth. Kathy gained a deeper sense of her Self, and she was forced through this experience to take a long hard look at the type of relationship she truly desired. She had also met some incredibly strong and powerful friends through their relationship, and these people remained her friends even after she at last divorced her husband.

Kathy also realized that she had carried around a vision of her life and the marriage she wanted; she was attempting to shove her ex-husband into this mold even though he was a round peg in the square hole of her vision. Kathy now realized she had been keeping herself closed off from people because she was afraid of being hurt again, and that she had been losing out on many wonderful intimate moments—opportunities for the kind of intimacy she longed for from her friends and family.

My friend then called her ex-husband on the phone right then and there and asked his forgiveness for blaming him all these years for how he had treated her. She explained that she had carried around all this anger for him, she had told her story of what a terrible person he was to everyone who would listen, and she had closed herself off to him even as a friend. She apologized and asked his forgiveness.

In reply, he told her he didn't want anything to do with her. He told her that she had hurt him beyond repair, and he asked her never to contact him again in any way, shape, or form. She agreed to abide by his wishes. Although he claimed Kathy hurt him, he was responsible for his participation in their relationship and his interpretation thereof. Her ex-husband often projected his guilt onto someone else in a feeble attempt to avoid taking responsibility for his participation. Kathy understood this and accepted him just the way he is, without worrying about how he chose to deal with this situation.

After that phone call, I asked her to tell me her story about their relationship again. This time, instead of the long, drawn-out drama I'd heard before, in which she was the victim of this terrible man, her new story was short and powerful. Kathy told me she had met this wonderful man (whom she later married). They'd had some great times and some not so great times. She told me how she tried to make him into something he wasn't, and how they both suffered through their experiences. Kathy told me how grateful she was for the entire experience and of the many blessings that she'd derived because of their relationship.

Finally, she told me she was saddened at the pain and fear he must have been experiencing to have done what he did, and the pain and fear he's still living with. But for all that, she was grateful for having known and loved him. The old story had been whiny, filled with her weak victimhood and her blame. The new story was powerful, full of responsibility, and it ended up with Kathy sharing a deep sense of gratitude.

Kathy told me she felt like a ton of bricks had been lifted off her chest, and she felt light and strong again. During the next few months, I noticed a different person—one stronger, more open, and more willing to share herself at depth—begin to emerge from within my dear friend. Recently Kathy told me that our earlier two-hour-long conversation literally changed her life. Seeing her relationship with her ex-husband in a different way, taking responsibility, refusing to be the victim anymore, and shifting her blame to gratitude has given her a whole new perspective on many aspects of her life. I'm so proud of my friend, Kathy.

You see, whenever we're holding anger, blame, and resentment against anyone else we're causing our bodies to deteriorate. Anger causes our bodies to generate chemicals that increase our heart rate, increase the blood pressure, and give us a heightened sense of awareness. This reaction was designed to help us survive threats to our physical bodies. Prolonged exposure to these chemicals causes our immune systems to become overwhelmed. The body was designed to flush these chemicals from our system in a short period of time. When we hold on to our anger, we keep flooding our bodies with these chemicals. Our body soon loses its ability to flush these chemicals out and they saturate the body. This overexposure eventually will lead to a severe weakening, and sometimes a complete collapse, of our immune systems. Anger kills, plain and simple.

Furthermore, whenever we're holding this anger in, we're playing the victims; we're refusing to take responsibility for our lives. Any situations that cause us long-term anger are the direct result of our being the victims and refusing to accept responsibility for our lives. Yet, we will bear the ultimate responsibility anyway, through deteriorating health and closed-off emotions.

So claim the power that's yours—take responsibility and clean up old angry situations. Accept your role in the situation, ask your partner (in the situation, not necessarily your partner in love) for forgiveness, and then find the lessons and the good in what's happened. **Clean the experience and story up, and live from an experience of love and empowerment. Shifting this one area of your life will free your body and your emotions up for you to experience exponentially greater spiritual and emotional growth.**

Take a long hard look at the interpretation, the story, you wrote about your circumstances and your experiences. Just as if you were writing a play or a movie, if you don't like the way the current script turns out, then rewrite it. Rewrite the interpretation of the events in your life so that you're empowered, so that these experiences fill your life with wonderful lessons, and so that you feel good about your Self.

You can literally change your past by merely choosing different interpretations! Because how we look at what happens in our lives is subjective, all interpretations are equally valid. So the question to ask your Self is, "Which one serves to empower me to live the life I most desire?"

### Take risks

Part of accepting the responsibility for your life is gaining the understanding that you're a human being, and as such, you're *designed* to make mistakes. Mistakes are oppor-tunities for you to learn about your Self and your life. Mistakes are an integral part of learning what you want and don't want in your life.

No person on this planet has ever been born with any such book or instinct as a *Universe Operator's Manual to Living As a Human Being.* Nobody knows everything there is to know about life. That's why we live our lives—to learn, to make mis-takes, to correct them, and then out of these lessons to experience lives filled with joy and love. You'll get no value from judging your Self, blaming your Self, or otherwise feeling bad about making mistakes. You may feel a little foolish if you

Crisis precedes transforma-tion. Before every quantum change, "problems" emerge—limits to growth, stagnation, unmanagable complexity, impending catastrophes, disin-tegration. From the perspec-tive of the present, the crisis looks like mistakes, deadly errors in the system. But from the perspective after the quan-tum transformation, these problems are seen to be "evo-lutionary drivers," vital stimu-lants which trigger astounding "design innovations." [9]

— Barbara Marx Hubbard

keep making the same mistakes over and over, failing to learn any les-son from these mistakes. Even this behavior is not wrong or bad; it just doesn't serve you to experiencing a life filled with Self-love.

Accept your mistakes as an integral part of life and learning. Use each experience as a foundation from which to redirect your beliefs and behav-iors into those that will deliver your heart's desires. Know that you are lovable even in the midst of making mistakes; after all, you're only human.

**The only people who don't make any mistakes are those who do nothing, and I might suggest that doing nothing is the most significant mistake of all.** Anyone who makes any decisions, anyone who actively participates in life in any way, anyone who's still breathing makes mis-takes. Also, those people who don't make any decisions *are* making mistakes, by refusing to live life. Don't be afraid to take the risk; you may or may not succeed on your first try. If you don't, then pick yourself back up, brush off your clothes, get back on your horse, and try again with your newfound knowledge.

*Don't be afraid to take risks.* Often we half-heartedly attempt things and then give up or sabotage our efforts as soon as we hit the slightest road-blocks. Doing this is another way of attempting to not take responsibility for trying and risking failure. By try-ing half-heartedly or by sabotaging ourselves, we're allowing our Selves off the hook. Then when we fail, we

. . . [B]eing one with the Tao, when you seek, you find; and when you make a mistake, you are forgiven.

That is why everybody loves it.[10]

— *Tao Te Ching,* Chapter 62

can blame the lack of effort or the sabotaging behavior. But we never really risk seeing whether or not we would have succeeded or would have failed.

Pay Attention to this behavior, because it's sneaky. If you really try, if you put your heart and soul into your efforts, then I guarantee you'll feel good about your Self, even if you don't achieve all that you want. The lessons you will learn along the way are often worth more than you could ever imagine, and often those lessons will ensure that you'll get what you seek the next time.

## Finding your lessons

I lead numerous seminars on how to achieve Self-love. During these workshops, I've often been asked, "How do I know what to do? How will I know what lessons I need to learn to live the life I truly desire?"

Let me say right away: *This isn't something you need to spend even one nanosecond being concerned about.* We live in an incredibly magical Universe. **The entire Universe was designed so that you'll know exactly when you're living your life from love and when you're living your life from fear.**

**Whenever you make a commitment to live your life in a certain way, the Universe—like magic—will immediately begin showing you all the areas in your life you need to clean up and heal in order to live that life.** All the lessons, all the opportunities to clearly see your fear-based beliefs will be provided to you on a silver platter. If you take one moment to step back from the day-to-day aspects of your life and look at your life to see where you're experiencing anything less than your dreams, those are the areas that you are living from a belief of fear. In those areas, your beliefs are causing you to create conditions of pain and suffering. Whenever you find any area of your life that's not 100 percent overflowing with joy, you are living from fear, and you have the opportunity to transform that aspect of your life from pain to joy.

When I began my journey, I made the commitment to live my life in absolute, complete honesty. While I didn't in the least consider myself a dishonest person then, the Universe quickly responded to my commitment anyway, by showing me every single aspect of my life, even areas I had been unaware of, in which I wasn't being absolutely, completely honest. I began to see where I wasn't telling the entire truth; perhaps I was telling someone what I thought they could handle or what I thought they wanted to hear. But you are either telling the truth or you're not. Just like you can't be a little bit pregnant, you can't be a little bit honest. I also immediately saw each and every instance in which I wasn't being absolutely, completely honest.

For instance, sometimes I wasn't telling people what I was really thinking; I was remaining quiet at times when my heart really had something to share. Dishonesty can take many forms. If you only tell part of the truth, and not the whole truth, you're being dishonest. If you withhold the truth from someone, you're being dishonest. Pretty soon, I clearly recognized each and every instance in which I wasn't living from absolute and complete honesty. While I was less than completely thrilled with each new discovery of my dishonesty, I was later amazed and joyous over this journey. As I began to address each of these areas, I soon experienced myself in an entirely new light. I began to trust myself—and I found I could increasingly trust others (for all people around us are "mirrors" of sorts, reflecting how we feel about ourselves).

> **Like magic, the Universe will always show you what you need to learn to advance to the next level, to drive towards living the life you most desire.**

Don't allow challenging opportunities like these to pass; don't shrink from the challenges; stand in the midst of them, find the lessons in them, learn from them, grow and keep your Self open. Soon you'll have the life you really desire and are committed to. **Life will only give you what you ask for; so don't be afraid to ask for the moon and the stars—they're yours for the asking!** Know that you'll have every opportunity to learn the lessons required for you to live your life in the clouds. It's all your choice.

## Owning your feelings

One of the most powerful aspects of Taking Responsibility is accepting ownership of your feelings, and knowing that it's absolutely perfect to feel however you feel. **One of the keys to having successful intimate relationships, romantic or platonic, is the ability to own your feelings and to take responsibility for those emotions.**

Too often we expect our partners to be mind readers, to interpret what we're attempting only indirectly to tell them—and then we hold them accountable when they fail to understand us! This is one of the greatest causes of friction and frustration between people. While it's going on, the person who's refusing to take responsibility for his wishes or comments is telling him Self he doesn't deserve to be heard.

Too often we refuse to accept ownership for what we want, thinking that if we just dare to ask directly the other person will turn us down, and we'll interpret this as still another sure sign that we aren't lovable.

> **Taking responsibility for your desires and feelings allows you to demonstrate the value of your Self.**

The truth of the matter is just the opposite. When we refuse to own our feelings or wishes, we are telling our Self that we don't deserve to be heard, we don't deserve to have our wishes come true. A couple of relatives of mine provide examples of this truth whenever we get together.

This husband and wife are truly wonderful, loving people who have the biggest, most generous hearts possible. They developed their habit of not owning their feelings some six decades ago, and by now it's just second nature to them. I accept them and love them just the way they are, and it certainly isn't my job to fix anyone else on this planet. But anyway, an example that illustrates this lesson happened just the other evening.

The woman in this couple wanted to have me help her carry a heavy box in from her car to my house. But instead of just outright asking me, she said, "It would be wonderful if someone in this house would help me carry something in from the car." Now I easily translated what she was really asking and jumped to volunteer to help her. She's a wonderful lady who doesn't feel comfortable enough in her Self to just ask me, "Grant, would you please carry the box in the back seat of the car into the house?"

Can you see it? When she asks indirectly that way, she's telling her Self that she doesn't deserve to have her desires come true. Some examples aren't so easy to translate. Since I Pay Attention and understand what is happening, whenever I don't easily understand what either one of this pair means, I ask *him or her* directly.

A slightly different example comes from another friend of mine. When someone asks her if she wants to do this or that, she simply makes no decision, or says something like, "I'm not entirely opposed to doing this." This is just her way of not making the decision but forcing the other person to make the decision, thus also forcing the other person to Take Responsibility for that decision.

You can really get a good read on how you're handling this area of your life by watching your words. If you use phrases like "We could . . ." or "If you really want, we could . . ." or "I wouldn't be entirely opposed to . . ." then you're attempting to sneakily avoid taking responsibility for your own feelings and choices. If you use phrases or sentences other than "I want . . ." or "I prefer . . ." or "I think . . ." or "I feel . . ." then you're not taking ownership of what you feel or want, and thus you are not taking responsibility for your Truth.

**Taking Responsibility is a positive, proactive way to tell your Self that you're worthy of being heard, worthy of having your feelings taken into consideration, and worthy of being loved enough to be respected for what you feel and think.** If you are not willing to accept ownership and responsibility for your own feelings, wants, and desires, then you're telling your Self that you really don't deserve to have these feelings, wants, and desires honored and accepted. In doing so, you're telling your Self that you are not worthy and not lovable enough to be listened to and honored.

I'm sure you know as well as I do: Nobody likes to be treated that way. That's why we all get so upset and angry when we think someone important to us isn't listening to us or taking us seriously. We naturally interpret such actions as "They don't care what I think or feel" or "They don't respect me enough to listen."

Take a positive step towards experiencing Self-love. Take Responsibility for Your Experience and your life. When you begin to take responsibility for your Self, you begin to demonstrate Self-respect and Self-love. You're worthy. You're lovable, even when you make mistakes. Every person on this planet experiences failures, letdowns, and drawbacks. These are not important. What is important is what we choose to do about these experiences.

Taking Responsibility for your Self, use these experiences as lessons that allow you to grow and expand. Each step you take will generate more and more positive feelings about your Self. You climb a mountain one step at a time; and you'll rebuild your Self-love the same way. Soon your efforts will allow you to experience positive, loving feelings for your Self. You'll gain a deeper sense of peace of heart and mind. Taking Responsibility allows you to transform destructive experiences into constructive, positive building lessons.

Take Responsibility for Your Experiences, claim the power that's yours to create the life you most desire. You can rewrite your past and the story about it, literally changing your interpretation about what happened (or didn't happen). When you change your interpretation of any situation, you'll change your experience of that event.

**Begin to live a great childhood today, regardless of what happened in the past. Create a memory that empowers you to create a life filled with Self-love and Self-respect. Become as a child. Live your life filled with wonder and awe at your magical Universe. Feel free to be powerful in expressing your desires and your emotions, and in claiming your good.**

# Spiritual Truths Discussed in this Chapter

**There is no right, there is no wrong, there is only that which serves you to create the life you most desire, or that which doesn't.**

Don't look at your prior life's experiences as opportunities for you to pass judgment on your Self. Look at these experiences as opportunities for you to learn about your Self and your life. Take each event and its circumstances, find the lesson, and be grateful for the Universe providing you with an opportunity to learn how to live a greater life.

**Playing the role of the victim means you're refusing to claim the power to change your life.**

As long as you play the role of the victim and blame someone or something else for your demise, then you'll continue to live a life filled with struggle and pain.

**Taking responsibility for your experiences gives you the power to change your life towards experiencing Self-love.**

If you blame someone or something else for your situation, then you're playing the role of the victim. If someone or something else created your life for you, then only they have the power to change it. Claim the power to live your life the way you choose. Take responsibility for your experience, and find an interpretation that empowers you to live the life you most desire.

**You can't avoid responsibility for your life; whatever your beliefs and behaviors are will dictate how you experience your life.**

A human being can never avoid Taking Responsibility for his or her life. Our lives are direct results of the choices we make. We alone have to live our lives and experience the conditions our choices have created. Pretending we're avoiding responsibility doesn't matter—we're always completely accountable for our thoughts, behaviors, and life experiences.

**Like magic, the Universe will always show you what you need to learn to advance to the next level, to drive towards living the life you most desire.**

The Universe is a magical place. The Universe will always provide you with the opportunity to learn every lesson you're required in order to live the life you desire.

**Taking responsibility for your desires and feelings allows you to demonstrate the value of your Self.**

When you claim your responsibility, when you claim the power in your life, you are proactively demonstrating to your Self that you deserve to have a great life. Build new habits of demonstrating your Self-love, and soon you'll feel that love flowing through your life.

$I$f you want to know the pattern of how you think, listen to how you speak habitually. It's how you speak habitually that counts. It really tells you how you think and feel about any given idea, if you listen to yourself.[1]

— Stretton Smith

## Chapter Five

# Speak Your Truth

The third "secret" or principle for generating the habit of treating your Self with love and Self-respect is to *Speak Your Truth*. Like each of the other principles, this concept is very simple and yet sometimes not so easy to adhere to. As you go through your life, your heart and soul yearn to share your Self. And when you deny your Self this opportunity, you are in essence telling your Self that you don't deserve to be heard. When you either withhold your true feelings, or you say anything that's not completely honest, you're telling your Self you're not lovable enough to be honored.

Many people on this planet have developed habits of not telling their Truth, either by not sharing themselves or by telling lies of varying degrees. Although we all pay lip service to honesty, dishonesty is rampant throughout our society. Much of this dishonesty is not only socially acceptable, but somewhat expected. I've often heard that it's not polite to directly ask someone else for a favor or a gift, even if that's something that your heart deeply desires. I was taught as a child that it's not polite to speak critically of anyone else. I heard the saying many times as a young child, "If you don't have anything nice to say, don't say anything at all."

While I subscribe to the concept of not degrading anyone else or speaking negatively towards or about someone else and not gossiping about other people, there are times that warrant clearly spoken, honest assessment. I've worked in several corporate cultures that consider even telling people they're wrong, even when you're sure of your facts, quite rude and inappropriate. I found that, in a culture like this, many decisions end up based on incorrect facts and assumptions because it's not socially acceptable to correct co-workers.

But lest we pat ourselves on the back, don't we, on an almost daily basis, tell our friends we "love" their haircuts, even when we really think they look terrible? We tell each other that purse, those shoes, or the color of that new car are all "great choices," even when we strongly feel the opposite. Many of us tell either direct bold-faced lies or so-called "white lies" in order to avoid confrontations or making others feel uncomfortable.

Politics and sales are professions where lack of honesty seems almost endemic. But we don't have to be politicos or high-pressure sellers to lie. We lie to the Internal Revenue Service, and we lie when we get pulled over by local law enforcement: "Gee, I'm sorry officer, I didn't see that speed limit sign." Dishonesty is rampant in our society, and each time we indulge in it, we're telling our Selves we don't deserve to have our Truth heard—or we're telling our Selves that we wouldn't be loved if the truth about us were really known.

## What we tell our Selves

Just as treating your Self with respect and love is a habit that's worth the effort to learn, honesty is also a habit well worth your effort to learn. **Being completely honest in every situation is one of the greatest methods of all to treat your Self with honor and respect. Displaying dishonesty in any situation is one sure way to tell your Self you don't deserve to be heard, or that you won't be lovable if someone knows the truth about you or the situation.**

**The Truth is, you are lovable, even when you're in the midst of doing unlovable acts.** Each and every one of us occasionally (and some more than others) acts out our fears. When this happens, even the most wonderful person alive can act in an unloving and inappropriate manner.

Let's take a look at how dishonesty can operate in our lives. There are three types of dishonesty. The first type is *withholding*. Whenever we have something to share with another person but we don't, we're telling our Selves that we don't deserve to be heard. This is, in essence, telling your Self that you're not lovable or that you don't deserve to be heard.

Your heart and soul deeply yearn to share your Self in this world, and you're dishonoring them when you withhold your Self. Every time you encounter a situation in your life and feel the desire to share your feelings, yet don't, you damage your sense of Self-love. Every time you feel the desire to share yourself and don't,

> The soul's communication of truth is the highest event in nature, since it then does not give somewhat from itself, but gives itself, or passes into and becomes that man whom it enlightens; or in proportion to the truth he receives, it takes him to itself.[2]
>
> — Ralph Waldo Emerson

102

you're in essence telling your Higher Self that you don't deserve to be heard, you don't deserve to be honored for how you feel.

Can you see how, when behaving this way, we're telling our Higher Selves that our feelings, thoughts, and ideas aren't worthy of being heard and considered by others? Because how we feel about our Selves is a direct reflection of how we treat our Selves, it's easy to understand why whenever we do this to ourselves many of us don't feel particularly lovable or worthy of being loved.

Now, I've never met anyone who hasn't withheld himself or herself (from sharing inner feelings or thoughts) at one time or another during his or her life, so please don't be too hard on your Self if you recognize this pattern in your life. Again, this is still another example of the principle, "What You Express, You Experience." When you encounter an event (or circumstance) and feel you've something to share or contribute, if you don't share yourself out of fear, then that's exactly what you're going to experience—fear.

Let Mike share a little of his story to bring this point home:

*When I was young, my father had a hair-trigger temper. You could never tell what would send him into a rage; even the most insignificant level of confrontation might result in a multi-hour tirade in which I ended up being hit and screamed at. Given this environment, I learned to do whatever it took to avoid anything that might resemble a confrontation. One of my defense mechanisms was lying. If a situation arose that I feared might lead to confrontation, I lied to avoid the situation. I'd say almost anything to avoid even the slightest semblance of a confrontation.*

*Even as an adult, whenever I've encountered any situation in life that might cause a confrontation, I've given in and shirked away instead. Yet each time something happened and I didn't stand up for myself, I could feel myself become tense and upset. I could feel my heart race, sweat break out on my forehead, and a deep sense of shame roll over me because I hadn't stood up for myself. I can't tell you how many times I ate incorrectly prepared food (like, cooked too much or too little) at restaurants because I didn't feel worthy enough to send it back. Yet every time this would happen, I'd feel smaller and less important, and more and more insecure about myself.*

*Once I recognized this pattern, I began to make a concerted effort to handle confrontations in an open, constructive manner. Now, I stand up for myself each time, and I feel better and stronger about myself. Just the other day I went to pick up some clothes at the laundry, and saw that they had torn one of my shirts. The old Mike would have just accepted the shirt, not said anything, and felt terrible and unimportant for not saying anything. But this time I quietly pointed out the tear in the shirt to the manager and confidently asked him to reimburse me the cost to replace it. After a few minutes of discussion, he agreed. I walked out of that shop feeling great. I've begun to feel like I do deserve to be treated well, and I've begun to feel strong and positive about myself. I now don't allow anyone to treat me worse than I want to be treated.*

The reason Mike started to feel his heart race, his brow break out in sweat, and a strong physical reaction is because this is the soul and body's message to us that we're not honoring our Selves. The human body reacts strongly to events in which we withhold our Selves or whenever we don't tell the truth. If you're dishonest, the body reacts to the dishonesty by increasing the adrenaline in your system and causing an increase in blood pressure, increasing your awareness and tenseness in your body, and resulting in faster breathing.

This reaction suggests that the soul and the body understand, at a deeper level than the mind, that dishonesty at any level is not an appropriate or natural behavior. This reaction is another way in which your body is sending you a message that you're out of alignment with loving your Self. This reaction is the basis for polygraph (lie-detector) machines, which measure heart rate, blood pressure, and breathing. When you're not telling the truth, your body reacts and the machine detects this condition.

Yesterday evening, a friend named Nisha (not her real name) called me from her office, even though it was almost 10:30 at night. I asked Nisha how she was doing, and she told me about some of her frustrations at work. She was working for a manager who was asking her to perform tasks within time frames that required her to work well into the evenings, while the manager would leave early each day.

> The Spiritual Value of Truth involves seeing things as they really are, avoiding denial, manipulation, and dishonest behavior that stops us from seeing or facing reality. It is the honest acceptance of who we are, and how we are in the world. Some call it integrity or honesty.[3]
> — Father Leo Booth

This left Nisha feeling used and abused. First thing each morning, her manager would inspect Nisha's work from the day and night before. Several times this past week, although she'd stayed up almost all night working, Nisha hadn't finished the assigned task. During the morning reviews the manager became very upset about the unfinished work. Nisha felt very frustrated, angry, upset, and unappreciated.

Nisha and I discussed the situation further, and I asked if she'd told her manager yet how she felt. Nisha confessed she had not, for fear of a confrontation. I suggested that perhaps a confrontation was warranted and might serve to clear the air, if it were done respectfully and constructively. Nisha agreed and promised to talk to her manager the very next morning.

Next day in her manager's office, Nisha told him she was working diligently and working very long hours, and yet she didn't feel the least bit appreciated. She suggested that she felt she was going above and beyond the call of normal work duty and still wasn't getting the work done, not because she wasn't putting forth the effort, but because the time frames were unreasonable. Finally, she asked her manager's help in figuring out this problem.

Nisha told me that the manager sat still for a moment, considered how to respond, and then after a few moments apologized to her. Apparently he was getting pressure from his bosses, and he felt he needed to respond to the pressure as promptly as possible. He explained that he was having to leave early each evening because he had a sick child at home who needed his care (he was a single parent). He apologized for not having recognized Nisha's situation and for not treating Nisha more appropriately. He also promised to give Nisha more help in her assignments and asked her to let him know if she still couldn't get the tasks done within reasonable business hours.

Nisha called me this afternoon to thank me. She said she was feeling great about herself again. She was much relieved at having stood up for herself and having cleared the air with her manager. She told me she was really angry at herself for not having either just left on time and not done the work, or for not telling her manager that he was being unfair. I suggested that the latter approach works much more positively with managers. I could hear the new lightness and confidence in her voice. When she was allowing herself to be treated poorly, she was telling her Self that this was the way she deserved to be treated. When she stood up for her Self, she was telling her Self that she was valuable and deserved to be treated with respect and honor. This is the way the Universe works.

The second type of dishonesty involves what I refer to as *active lies*. This type of dishonesty is the easiest to recognize and to understand. When you look another person in the face and tell them anything you know isn't true, you're actively being dishonest. Once again, being dishonest is another way of telling your Self you don't deserve to be heard or that no one would love you if they knew the truth about you. Many people who've developed the habit of active dishonesty get caught in vicious cycles so that it becomes seemingly impossible for them to escape. Melinda shares her experience learning this tough lesson:

> Because I felt unlovable as a child and throughout my early adult years, I used to lie about my various accomplishments and feats in order to make myself look better in the eyes of my friends and co-workers. I exaggerated my feats as an athlete and as a scholar. I used to tell people I wanted to impress that I was the head cheerleader of my high school and all sorts of other things I thought would make me look good in their eyes.

*These lies became a vicious cycle. What I most wanted was to know that I was lovable for who I was, that someone really cared about who I was just because of who I am. I could never trust that someone could ever love me for me, so I lied. At first these were silly, fairly harmless fibs, but later they became more elaborate, and soon they became part of my identity. Yet when I told these lies in order to make myself seem more lovable, and then someone told me he or she did love me, I couldn't believe them. I couldn't believe they would love me for who I was instead of the image of the person I'd worked to create.*

*Several of my friends have since told me they could tell when I wasn't telling the truth—whenever I didn't look them in the eyes as I was speaking to them. The soul understands the significance of lies, and one of the signals it sends out is the inability to look another person directly in the eye when you're lying. Many people could either see through my lies or sense that I wasn't being honest with them. So they didn't trust me. They certainly didn't extend their trust or their love to a person who was constantly lying to them. It felt like I was damned if I didn't lie, and damned if I did. At the end of the day, I never felt like anyone would ever love me, no matter what.*

*Once I fully understood what I was doing to myself, I made the commitment to relearn and start a new habit, a habit of being completely honest. I was going to be me, I was going to be honest about who I was, and I was going to let people get to know the real me. I stopped telling lies, on any and all levels, and soon people learned to trust me again. More importantly, I began to trust myself. People sensed this new openness and honesty, and soon they began to open and share themselves with me on deeper and more intimate levels. My relationships became richer, fuller, and more intimate. Now, I can honestly say that my life is filled with people who know me and love the true me for just who and what I am. This has become an incredible transformation; I now have my life back.*

The third and final type of dishonesty is *passive lies*. I've often heard people attempt to justify partial truths or "little white lies." Yet whenever you only tell someone part of the truth, you're passively telling a lie. Although that partial thing you're telling him is truthful, by withholding the rest of the truth from him you're misleading him or allowing him to draw an interpretation or conclusion you know to be false; in other words, you're being dishonest.

(Jesus said)

*Listen to the word, understand knowledge, and love life. Then no one will persecute you and no one will oppress you, unless you do this to yourselves.*[4]

— *The Secret Book of James*, Chapter 5:8

Sometimes when you're telling another person what you believe is true at the moment, as soon as you discover that you told him something that was false, then it serves you to reconnect with him and inform him of your discovery. Doing so, you ensure that everything you tell anyone is truthful at the moment, and continues to be truthful even later.

> **Withholding one's Self, participating in active or passive lies—all these are different methods of being dishonest.**

Any amount or level of dishonesty, regardless of which type or degree, is still dishonesty. This is one issue that's either black or white, with no shades of gray in between. There is no middle ground when dealing with honesty, nor is there middle ground in the message you're sending your Self. Even if you're being a "little" dishonest, you're being completely dishonest. If you're just a smidgen untruthful, then you're not being honest. Either you're completely honest or you're not, plain and simple.

When you don't tell the absolute truth, you're telling your Self you're not lovable. Only when you feel strong enough to tell the absolute truth, and know you're lovable in the midst of that truth, will you send a strong demonstration to your soul and your Self that you're lovable.

> **Either you're completely honest or you're dishonest. There is no middle ground.**

Any level of dishonesty results in telling your Self that you're not lovable. Regardless of how your dishonesty manifests itself, any level or type of dishonesty results in sending the message to your Self that you're not lovable.

### The Truth will set you free

Learning and developing a new habit of always being honest will set you free from the bondage of the belief that you're not lovable. Honesty also will free you from looking over your shoulder, wondering when someone is going to catch you

> (Jesus said),
> *And ye shall know the truth, and the truth shall make you free.*
> — *Gospel of John* 8:32

in a lie. Learning to be honest and practicing absolute honesty will free you from feeling you're not worthy or lovable. It will free you from feeling that people won't respect or love you if you speak your mind or if people learn the truth about you.

You see, **being dishonest directly tells your Self you're not worthy to be heard, you're not worthy of respect, and you're not lovable. When we continually tell our Selves that we aren't lovable, our Selves begin to believe this message.** This message becomes ingrained in our psyches, and we then interpret the world through the filter of "I'm not lovable," and everything we see, hear, and read begins to give us more and more validation of that belief. One of the strongest ways to break this cycle and begin to learn the true value of your Self is to learn the new habit of being absolutely honest.

### Speaking and sharing your truth demonstrates to your Self that you're lovable.

To honor and respect your Self, to demonstrate the Self-love you wish to experience in your daily life, you must be willing to be completely open and honest in all situations. One caveat adheres to this principle: Apply this rule when and where it serves you, not on an indiscriminate basis. Share what is in your heart and in your soul, not just whatever pops into your brain. Many silly and sometimes less-than-nice thoughts pop into my brain on a daily basis, like, "Boy, that's one ugly pair of blue, pink, and green plaid slacks that man's wearing," or, "Who in his right mind would buy an aquamarine Ferrari?" These thoughts should be filtered and not shared, because sharing these thoughts won't serve anyone. These thoughts aren't from your heart; rather they're from the fear-based part of the brain. Sharing from the heart and the soul always generates love, and sharing thoughts and feelings from your heart and soul won't hurt another person's feelings or Self-esteem.

I grew up in a childhood environment somewhat similar to Mike's. I learned that it was safer to not always be honest. I grew up with a terrible sense of my own Self-esteem and an incredible lack of Self-love. But when I discovered these five principles and began to exercise the principle of honesty, my Self-esteem immediately began to grow stronger and healthier. Immediately I made the commitment to always tell the truth, regardless of the consequences. The Universe—like magic—then began to show me every single area in my life where my dishonesty was embedded. As I began to Pay Attention to what I was saying in each of these areas, I noticed how easily I tended to lie and how hard it was to sometimes deal with situations from complete honesty.

As I Paid Attention to all my words and action, as I began to Take Responsibility for all my words and actions, I immediately began to sense a change in my life. I immediately began to see myself as someone who wasn't a liar, but rather as someone everyone could trust to always tell the truth (and also to always do what I said I was going to do). The way we treat others is a mirror of how we feel about ourselves. As I began to transform my feelings towards Self-love, I began to be capable of having much richer and deeper relationships with the people in my life. I learned to trust and learned to love my Self.

When we do decide to open our hearts and mouths and share what we truly think and feel, it seems like a giant weight lifts off us. There have been times in my life when I didn't share my feelings and I withheld what was in my heart. When this was happening, I could literally feel myself generating a heaviness in my heart. I felt walls being built up around me and trust in relationships eroding away. When I decided to share what was going on in my heart, I felt instantaneously lighter and as if the walls had been torn down. The one and only way you can transform these kinds of feelings of distrust and distance back into trust and intimacy is by openly sharing your heart. Deep, honest communication tears these walls down and rebuilds trust almost immediately. This is the key to having great relationships: completely open and honest communication.

Although I've made a commitment to myself to live from complete honesty, I do find that sometimes words will slip from my mouth that might be interpreted as less than completely honest. At such times I can almost see the words slip out of my mouth and past my lips, and I watch as my soul wants to reach out and literally grab them back in midair before they reach anyone else's ears. When this happens, I immediately know that some fear is stirring inside me, and I need to take a step back, find out where it is, and address that fear head on.

I also immediately take complete accountability and responsibility for my words and attempt as soon as possible to rectify the situation with all parties involved. Sometimes I find that I've said something I thought was true at the time, only to find out later that my words were inaccurate. I then also take responsibility and make every effort to set the record straight with anyone who was involved. Because I do this, all my friends and family always know they can absolutely count on me to tell the truth, to be totally and absolutely honest at all times. They have nothing to fear from me, and they know I'm never hiding anything from them. Experiencing these feelings, my sense of Self-love and Self-esteem are instantaneously transformed.

**Take Responsibility for your life. Speak Your Truth. Feel the love you have in your heart begin to fill your life. Watch your life be transformed from pain and suffering to joy and love. Learn to see the world through new eyes. Become as a child. Experience all the joy and wonder the Universe has to offer, without having to look over your shoulder. Know that you're an incredible person, because you're divine.**

# Spiritual Truths Discussed in this Chapter

**Withholding one's Self, participating in active or passive lies—all these are different methods of being dishonest.**

Both active lies and passive lives are forms of being dishonest. Participating in life dishonestly tells your Self you are not lovable if the truth becomes known. Being completely honest demonstrates that you're lovable in all situations.

**Either you're completely honest or you're dishonest. There is no middle ground.**

This is really like being "half pregnant" (there's no such condition); either you're completely honest or you're not. It's black and white, with no shades of gray in between.

**Speaking and sharing your truth demonstrates to your Self that you're lovable.**

Begin to build the habit of being completely honest. When you share your truth, you're proactively demonstrating to your Self that you're lovable and you deserve to be heard.

$T$his inner life is a world of thought; and thought promotes action. Now, as a man thinks, so he becomes— he is creating his inner world. From that inner world come his speech and action.[1]

— White Eagle

## Chapter Six

# Keep Your Agreements

The fourth "secret" or principle to experiencing Self-love is to *Keep Your Agreements*. This is the "action" portion of Speak Your Truth. By Keeping Your Agreements, you ensure that whatever you say is always the truth. Once again, when you make agreements and don't fulfill them you're telling your Self you don't deserve to be honored or respected.

> Your life works exactly to the degree that you keep your agreements. An Agreement has integrity because you make it, and for no other reason.[2]
>
> — Ron Smothermon, M.D.

Making and then breaking agreements is, in essence, the same as lying and has the same effect on your Self-esteem. You can't but help to feel bad—about your Self—when you continually make and break agreements. You destroy everyone's trust in you including the trust of your Self. When you make and then Keep Your Agreements, you honor your word, you honor your Self, and you build up your Self-esteem and Self-love.

Keeping Your Agreements sounds simple, but sometimes it's not. Like honesty, there is no middle ground here. Either you honor and fulfill your agreements or you don't. For example, you make an agreement to meet a friend at a particular place at 2:00 p.m. on Wednesday. If you're not at that exact spot before 2:01 p.m. on Wednesday, you're late and you didn't keep your agreement. If you show up and then blame your lateness on traffic, you're merely being the traffic's victim. You are still late, and you didn't honor your agreement. It's very simple—either you did or you didn't Keep Your Agreement. If your intention was to Keep Your Agreement, you would have started driving to meet your friend and given your Self enough time to factor in time for the traffic conditions. When you make the commitment to Keep Your time Agreements, you do whatever it takes to ensure that you're always either on time or early.

Or take your office agreements. If you make a commitment to turn in a certain assignment at a certain time, you only keep your agreement if you turn in the completed assignment on time. You also make an implied commitment to complete your assignments in ways acceptable to your position at the office. Once again, either you complete the assignment and Keep Your Agreement or you don't. "The dog ate my report" is an excuse, and even if it really happened, you still didn't Keep Your Agreement.

> **Keeping Your Agreements is the action part of Speaking Your Truth. When you Keep Your Agreements, you're telling your Self that you deserve to be honored and respected.**

When you fail to keep an agreement you've made, then Take Responsibility and move on. Say, "I'm sorry, I was late." That's Taking Responsibility, without blaming anyone or anything. If you blame someone or something else, what you're really telling your Self and the person you made the agreement with is that you're not willing to Take Responsibility, so this will happen again. If, on the other hand, you Take Responsibility, admit your error, and then reaffirm your commitment to Keep Your Agreements in the future, you begin to rebuild trust. The other person is much more likely to begin to reinvest his trust in you. The same goes for you—you'll maintain the trust you have in your Self.

Let's read about Melinda's experience in learning this lesson:

> *I always seem to be running late wherever I go. I begin each day with the thought that I want to keep on time, but within the first hour or so of every morning, I find myself running late. Then I run late to all my appointments all day long. I also feel like I can't say "no" to someone who asks me for a favor. I dread that if I tell him "no," he'll disapprove of me, and that would make me feel even worse about myself.*

> *This one particular morning I had an agreement with my mother to meet her at the mall at ten. I got up an extra fifteen minutes early to make sure I'd be there on time. One thing led to another and I left the house ten minutes late, and with heavy traffic I showed up almost fifteen minutes late. My mother very patiently reminded me of our agreement. She also told me that when I'm late to meet with her, it's like I'm telling her that my time is worth more than hers. She told me that it feels like I'm being disrespectful towards her. Mom told me she understands that we all have things going on in our lives, but that if I respected her I'd keep my agreements and show up on time.*

*I apologized and told her I understood what she was telling me. I then told her that the last thing I wanted to do was to give her any message that I didn't love her and didn't respect her. I cherish, love, and completely respect my mother. It hurt me to think I was giving her any message to the contrary.*

*We finished our conversation and spent a nice day shopping together. All during our time together at the mall, I was thinking about what my mother had said, how she felt I was telling her that I didn't respect her and that I was telling her my time was more valuable than hers. She was absolutely correct, and towards the end of the day I apologized to her again and told her that I really understood what she'd said to me. Right then and there I made myself a commitment to begin to Keep My Agreements. As soon as I made this commitment, one that I really intended on keeping this time, I began to feel better about myself.*

*I can really see that my friends and family have learned not to trust me whenever I've told them I was going to do something. My older sister has even gone so far as to tell me to meet her thirty minutes early, just to make sure that I would show up on time. Of course, even with this lead time, I'm usually still late. This isn't the person I want to be. I want to be a person who people know will keep her word, and when I say something, they'll automatically know it will be done.*

*Now, I leave with enough time to keep my commitments. I even account for some additional traffic problems. I've become someone that my friends, co-workers, and family can count on as always being on time and keeping my agreements. I do things when I say I'm going to get them done. And I can see the trust being rebuilt. I'm beginning to feel more trust towards myself. Before, I tended to make agreements I knew I couldn't keep. I'd feel badly even before I broke the commitments. Now, I know I will keep the agreements I make.*

*I've also developed a strong enough sense of Self-love to tell people "no" when they ask me for something either I don't want to do or I don't think I can do. That feels great. It feels like I'm sticking up for my Self, that I'm honoring my Self. I can feel the Self-esteem growing. I like trusting myself and seeing others around me trust me as well. It feels great.*

**As you begin to Keep Your Agreements, just as when you're learning the habit of always being honest, you will immediately see an increase in your Self-esteem and Self-love.** Your friends and family will learn to trust you, knowing that when you say something you'll follow through. You will begin to trust your Self, and you will instantaneously begin to feel better about your Self.

## Saying "no"

Another of the traps we often find our Selves in when we lack Self-love is not having the ability to say "no" when we're asked to do something. We feel that if we say "no," the person asking us won't love us. Although we know we either won't or can't fulfill her request, we agree to the request. Then we proceed on with our lives, and we fail to keep our agreement. Then we feel badly about not only failing to fulfill our commitments, we also feel badly about our Selves, because we know we've destroyed some of the trust of the person making the request. Pretty soon, our friends, our family, our co-workers, and our acquaintances all have lost trust in us. More importantly, we've lost trust in our Selves.

## Saying "no" allows you to Keep Your Agreements, and builds trust and respect.

When you make the commitment to always Keep Your Agreements, you'll also learn to make agreements only when you have the intention and ability to fulfill them. You'll be able to rebuild the trust of your friends and family. You'll also learn to keep clear communication about agreements, making sure both you and the other person in the agreement understand what was agreed to and what wasn't. People will quickly learn that you're trustworthy, and you'll do what you say. Then you'll begin to rebuild the trust in your Self. People will actually trust and respect you more when you learn to say "no" to them occasionally.

### Alignment

Once you begin living the commitment to always Keep Your Agreements, you'll then find that the Universe will "magically" align itself with you and create opportunities for you to complete your agreements with the least effort possible. Once you move into the consciousness of being a living demonstration of

> Every act of man has its origin in thought, which is expressed into the phenomenal world from a mental center that is but a point of radiation for an energy that lies back of it.[3]
>
> — Charles Fillmore

Self-love and Self-respect, you literally change the pattern of the energy that flows through you. This new energy attracts situations and circumstances that respond to your new thoughts.

When you make a commitment, the Universe will begin to align itself with you in Keeping Your Agreements. Lights will turn green so you can zip through crowded intersections. Traffic will spontaneously allow you to pass, or will be lighter than you expected. The Universe will begin the process, just because you said so. I'm not really sure how all this happens, but I invite you to begin to live from a commitment of Self-love; then you can expect to begin to experience it for your Self. Like I said, it seems and feels like magic. It's not; it's merely the Universe responding to your new beliefs, thoughts, and the new pattern of energy your consciousness has created.

Keep Your Agreements, rebuild the trust you have in your Self. Allow your co-workers, allow your friends and family to know you're trustworthy. Learn to trust your Self. Become strong in knowing you're a wonderful person. Become as a child. Know that you're living as a wonderful, loving, generous person. Experience loving your Self and sharing your Self openly and honestly in every aspect of your life.

# Spiritual Truths Discussed in this Chapter

**Keeping Your Agreements is the action part of Speaking Your Truth. When you Keep Your Agreements, you're telling your Self you deserve to be honored and respected.**

Keeping Your Agreements ensures that whatever you say comes true. It's the action portion of Speaking Your Truth. By Keeping Your Agreements, you rebuild trust in your Self for you and others. You become a living demonstration of your Self-love and Self-respect.

**Saying "no" allows you to Keep Your Agreements and builds trust and respect.**

Don't make commitments you either can't or won't keep. When it's done appropriately, saying "no" actually earns the respect of others. Only make agreements when you have the fullest intention of fulfilling the agreement. Demonstrate your Self-love by saying "no" when you need to.

$T$he Tao is like a bellows:

it is empty yet infinitely capable.

The more you use it, the more it produces.[1]

— *Tao Te Ching*, Chapter 5

## Chapter Seven

# Ask for What You Want

The fifth and last "secret" or principle to achieving Self-love is to *Ask for What You Want* and do so *When You Want It*. When you hold the belief you're not lovable, you don't honor your heart's desires by asking for them. Instead, when opportunity arises you often remain quiet.

Consider this: Every time you have a heartfelt desire for anything and don't take positive action, either in the form of a request or otherwise, to get it, you're telling your Self you

> Strength lies in the ability to ask boldly and give people freedom to accept or refuse, including yourself. The strong have no trouble saying no to things that would wear other people out. They know that life is a labor pain and that they are giving birth to themselves.[1]
>
> — Bernie Siegel, M.D.

don't deserve to have your desires fulfilled. But remember: You're an incredible person; you're divine at your very essence. You *deserve* to have all your heart's desires fulfilled as soon as you become aware of them.

Learn to boldly Ask for What You Want, When You Want It. Don't delay in your request, don't wait until later to ask. Ask when the desire makes itself known to you. Carpe Diem, Seize the Day, take advantage of the opportunities as they present themselves!

Why don't we Ask for What We Want more often? Because we're afraid of being rejected, afraid we'll be told "no." When you choose not to ask for what you really want, you're really rejecting your Self before the other person has the chance to say either "yes" or "no." But this guarantees 100 percent that you will be rejected, whereas if you take the risk, the probabilities of your getting what you want are surely significantly greater.

117

You often don't ask because you don't feel worthy to receive. Because you're unlovable, you don't deserve to have what you really want. Or so you believe about your Self. Hey—**nobody on this planet deserves to be happy more than you do. Know that you deserve to have all the greatest gifts on this planet effortlessly flow into your life. Know you deserve to have all your heart's desires fulfilled instantaneously.** Any other belief is a fear-based belief—an old habit that no longer serves you. Create a new habit in your life by boldly *Asking for What You Want, When You Want It.* Create a new habit for your life by demonstrating to your Self that you deserve to have your heart's desires fulfilled now.

> ## Asking for What You Want demonstrates to your Self that you deserve to have your heartfelt desires fulfilled.

I'm currently "owned by" two beautiful golden retrievers, Queen Maya (or Maya) and Joshua. They send me to work each day so I can earn enough money so they can lounge around the house and live lives of complete luxury, constantly pampered and smothered with affection and love. Their lives are great, consisting of eating, sleeping, playing, and being loved. They know what they want, and when they want something they boldly ask for what they want, when they want it.

My two dogs have never learned the fear of rejection. Whenever they want to be showered with affection, they gently nudge me with their noses or come to my side and lean into me. They both can be quite persistent when they choose. Last night I was trying to answer my e-mails when Maya wanted to be petted. She kept putting her snout under my arm and nudging; in fact she was adamant until I finally gave in.

I petted her for a minute or so and then tried to go back to my e-mails. But Maya wanted more. She just kept nudging my arm until I finally got on the floor with her and gave her a full-body rubdown for several minutes. She loves to lie on her back and have her belly vigorously rubbed, so that's just what I did. When she was finally satisfied, she rolled over and walked away a happy and contented pooch. Luckily, Maya is most hungry for affection in the morning, while Joshua wants to be fawned over and petted in the evening. This works out well so I can give each one my undivided attention. Both these dogs provide a great demonstration of Asking for What You Want, When You Want It—and not settling for less.

**Another magical aspect of the Universe is that you will receive the absolute least you're willing to settle for.** In your heart, you may desire to have a fifteen-foot schooner (sailboat). When you ask for this, the Universe usually comes back and offers a ten-foot sunfish (small sailboat). If you accept this gift, the Universe will cease to work to provide what you really desire, thinking it's fulfilled your request.

So be clear in your request—Ask for What You Want, When You Want It. Don't settle for less. The Universe will then tempt with you a slightly larger sailboat. Don't settle; you deserve to have all your heart's desires completely fulfilled. Once the Universe understands that you understand you deserve to have the best in your life, your wishes will be fulfilled with your desires or greater. I'm not sure how this happens, but time and time again this has been proven.

Of course, a certain amount of logic and common sense also applies with this principle. You must Pay Attention to what you're asking for. Many times, we think we're asking for one thing and we're really asking for something entirely different. When this happens, take a step back and make a new request, Asking for What You Want.

There is an old adage: "Be careful what you ask for; you just might get it." This adage applies here completely. You must be willing to Take Responsibility for whatever you ask for, because many times you'll get it. If your request is based on fear, then you'll generate pain and suffering from your expression of these fears. If your request is socially inappropriate or even criminal in nature, you'll have the opportunity to Take Responsibility for that behavior also.

If, for example, you walk into a bank and ask for all their money, then you might be given the money—temporarily. But you'll probably also have your room and board paid for you by the Department of Corrections for the next five to ten years. Before the law-enforcement officials catch you—and they catch virtually all major criminals—you'll have to live your life on the run, and always be looking over your shoulder. This doesn't seem like the life I would choose to live, and I hope the same goes for you.

This principle works, even if your request is inappropriate. You will, however, have to Take Responsibility for your behavior and therefore have the opportunity to learn a painful lesson if you choose this route. Pay Attention—if your request is made from love and because you're seeking greater opportunities to generate a better life for you and those around you (from a place of love), then your request will be fulfilled with the same love. Please remember: Fear-based thoughts and behaviors generate pain and suffering (either directly or indirectly). Love or faith-based thoughts always generate joy and bliss (either directly or indirectly).

### Desire is divine

When I've taught these principles, people who've learned that there somehow is nobility in poverty have often challenged me. Any level of material wealth and comfort seems to be against their religious teachings, because these folks believe that it's more divine to be poor than to have what you desire. In fact, many people have been taught that desires are "bad" or "wrong," regardless of what the desire is.

But that's not what the great spiritual teachers have taught. The great spiritual teachers insisted just the opposite—that abundance and prosperity are what God wishes for us. Let's look at their teachings in a little more detail.

Many people believe that "money is the root of all evil"; but as the Holy Bible's *Book of Timothy* 6:10 teaches us, ". . . the *love* of money is the root of all evil." Did you get that? It's the love of money that's the root of all evil, not the possession of money or material wealth itself. It's when we place the love of money above the love of our Selves, the love of our family, and the love of God that we're misplacing our values.

> In a comprehensive survey entitled *The Quality of American Life* published a decade ago, the authors report that a person's financial situation is one of the least important factors affecting overall satisfaction with life.[3]
>
> — Mihaly Csikszentmihalyi, Ph.D

If we believe for one moment that money or material possessions will give us happiness or peace of mind, we're sadly mistaken. Money will never give anyone happiness. Money will never give anyone peace of heart. Many times, the opposite seems true. When you have $1,000 you want $10,000. When you have $10,000, you want $100,000, and so on. Once you tie your sense of happiness with money or material wealth, you'll never have enough. We desire more and more because we think that the next "level" of possession will provide us the happiness that our current level of wealth didn't provide. While material wealth may provide a temporary sense of satisfaction at your accomplishment, it will never make you happy.

You'll never acquire enough money or "things" to find peace of mind or peace of heart; you'll never acquire enough to gain a sense of Self-love. A study of recent state lottery winners and how winning has affected them suggests that ninety-five percent of lottery winners say winning *ruined* their lives.[4] Almost everyone I know thinks winning the lottery will cure all their ills. I've also read recently that more than eighty percent of all lottery winners are bankrupt after three years—even those who were otherwise financially responsible before winning. The instant infusion of all that wealth actually destroys the lives of most of the winners. The winners suddenly had everyone asking them for loans, gifts, and charity. Pretty soon they didn't know who to trust and who not to trust. They fell into the same trap our movie stars and professional athletes do, without a safe place to invest their love. They ended up alone, frustrated, and miserable.

Money, material wealth in and of itself, doesn't generate happiness. Contrary to popular opinion, in most instances material wealth actually causes suffering and pain. The great spiritual teachers don't emphasize instant wealth; they emphasize that it's our divine nature to live a life filled with abundance and prosperity. This means we were created to live a life filled with all sorts of wealth: vitality and great health, wonderfully fulfilling relationships, material wealth, and Self-love.

In fact, the Bible tells us a remarkable story that illustrates this lesson well. King David (the great Jewish King) anointed his son, Solomon, to ascend to the throne and become king upon his death. Shortly after this proclamation, David passed away and Solomon was crowned King, God came to him and offered him anything he might desire. While many people might have asked for great wealth or everlasting life, Solomon asked God for "an understanding heart to judge thy people" (*First Book of Kings* 3:9).[2] God replied, "Behold, I have done according to thy words: lo, I have given thee a wise and an understanding heart; so that there was none like thee before thee, neither after thee shall any arise like unto thee. And I have also given thee that which thou hast not asked, both riches, and honour: so that there shall not be any among the kings like unto thee all thy days" (*First Book of Kings* 3:12-13).

If material wealth were so evil and if poverty were divine, then God would certainly not have rewarded King Solomon with more wealth than any other king has ever possessed, would He?

The Bible is actually filled with wonderful teachings in which God tells us that our Divine nature is one of abundance and prosperity. In the *Book of Psalms*, we're taught that the Lord will send us prosperity—**now**. If poverty were divine and prosperity were always an evil, then I doubt the Lord would have promised us prosperity. Furthermore, in the *Book of Malachi* (shown below) the priests taught that when you live with a generous heart and recognize the source of all your substance, then God will open up the windows of heaven and send so many blessings you can't imagine them all. In the only place in all the spiritual teachings where God asks us to "prove" Him, God tells us directly that when you actively demonstrate your faith He will shower you with untold wealth, so there won't be enough room to receive it all:

> This is the day which the LORD hath made; we will rejoice and be glad in it. Save now, I beseech thee, O LORD: O LORD, I beseech thee, send now prosperity.
>
> — *Book of Psalms* 118:24-25

> Bring ye all the tithes into the storehouse, that there may be meat in mine house, and **prove me now** herewith, saith the LORD of hosts, if I will not open you the windows of heaven, and pour you out a blessing, that there shall not be room enough to receive it.
>
> — *Book of Malachi* 3:10

---

[2] King Solomon is often referred to as Solomon the Wise because he chose wisdom and compassion rather than wealth.

The spiritual teachings also remind us that we're all Children of God, and that God is the energy of love. Any parent will naturally provide everything they can within their resources for their children. Then certainly God (whose love is far greater than our ability to understand) will do the same for His Children. I know that most of us love to share generously with children or even other people in

> And God is able to provide you with every blessing in abundance, so that you may have enough of everything and may provide in abundance for every good work.
>
> — *Second Letter to the Corinthians* 9:8

general. The joy and glee in their eyes fill our hearts with joy when they receive our presents.

Remember the story I told you of the time I decorated our house for Easter, and Kendall screamed with joy every time she found an Easter egg? Just the simple, pure joy in her eyes was enough to create such a wonderful memory and feeling within me that it became one of the great moments of my entire life. The same desire and joy to shower His Children is true with God.

Then why would anyone think God wouldn't want to shower us with the same gifts—why would God not want to experience the same love as He fills our lives with the treasures of the Heaven? Jesus tells us this is the case—that God loves to make sure our lives are filled with abundance and prosperity. It's only our consciousness that keeps the gifts from effortlessly flowing into our lives. In the *Gospel of Luke* 12:32, Jesus tells us to have faith that God will provide when he says, *"Fear not, little flock; for it is your Father's good pleasure to give you the kingdom."* We are Children of God and, as such, He loves to provide us with everything we need to live a life filled with abundance and prosperity.

## Spirit desires your life to be filled with prosperity.

Whole books are filled with the prosperity teaching of the Bible. And Judaism and Christianity aren't the only spiritual teachings that tell us about our divine nature as prosperous beings. The teachings of the *Tao Te Ching (Tao)* are entirely about prosperity. These teachings describe

> The supreme good is like water,
>
> which nourishes all things without trying to.[5]
>
> — *Tao Te Ching*, Chapter 8

the Universe as having a gentle flow of loving energy, like a gentle mountain stream winding its way down the side of the mountain. When we are out of alignment with our flow of life energy (*chi'*), then our lives will be filled with struggle and strife. We'll struggle against life just like we would have to struggle when paddling our boats upstream. However, when we align ourselves with the Universe's flow of energy, our lives will be filled with ease and joy (which is my definition of prosperity).

Chapter 5 of the *Tao Te Ching* says, "The Tao is like a bellows: it is empty yet infinitely capable. The more you use it, the more it produces."[6] The *Tao* also teaches that, once you understand the principles behind the Universe, you can use them to create whatever you desire in your heart; furthermore, the more you use these principles, the more you can produce. Much like exercising a muscle, the more you practice the principles, the more you can create the experience you most desire in your life. This principle teaches us that our prosperity is currently flowing into our lives; we just need to be aware of these gifts and feel worthy enough to receive them.

## Desire is God's way of telling you a gift is already on its way towards you.

Emilie Cady, the great metaphysician of the late 1800s, captured one of the most powerful spiritual concepts I've ever read. Emilie Cady was a physician who practiced and proved the spiritual principles in her everyday life. She wrote a series of short articles on metaphysical teachings

> Desire in the heart is always God tapping at the door of your consciousness with His infinite supply.[7]
>
> — H. Emilie Cady

that were later brought together in the book *Lessons in Truth.*

In this book, Emily teaches us that **our heartfelt desires are really God telling us to be aware that His gifts are already on their way to us.** If we didn't have these heartfelt desires, we wouldn't be aware of these opportunities (these treasures of heaven) when they presented themselves to us. Instead, by placing these desires in our hearts, God was ensuring we would be aware of our gifts as they naturally flowed into our lives. Once aware, we could then accept our gifts with gratitude.

**Don't be afraid to Ask for What You Want, When You Want It. Your heartfelt desires are divine. Your desires are God telling you that those gifts are already on their way to you, so be aware and make sure you grab them as they flow by. Your divine nature is one of abundance and prosperity. Boldly Ask for What You Want, When You Want It. Asking is the only way you allow the rest of us to know what your divinely inspired gifts are, so that we may be of service to provide them to you.**

### Detachment

When you Ask for What You Want, When You Want It, then do so with detachment concerning the outcome. Please remember, the person receiving your request also has complete free will. You have every right in the world to make a request, and the person on the receiving end has every right in the world to either fulfill your request or to deny it.

When Asking for What You Want, always keep this in mind: If you start asking everyone for everything with the mindset that you'll always receive everything you ask for, then you're setting your Self up for being frustrated and upset. Many times we don't know the channel Spirit has chosen to send our gifts; we merely feel the desire for the gift. Most of the time the channel we believe this gift will come through isn't the one chosen by Spirit. Spirit instead chooses to send us our gifts by the most unusual channels. Most of my gifts seem to come from left field. In fact, they come from the channel I'd least expect them to travel through. For example, I have often expected to get a nice bonus at work or a big raise. The Universe had other plans and instead funneled money to me through an inheritance.

Also, when you don't Ask for What You Want, you are denying the other person his or her ability to express generosity and love. **Because we only experience what we express, another person will only experience himself or herself as loving and generous when you create the opportunity for that person to give to you.** Once again, please remember: While we might think we know which channel (or which person) Spirit intends on using, we usually don't.

When practicing this principle, it will amaze you what people will be willing to either do for you or give you if you'll only ask. Last December I made a two-week trip out to California. While I was there, I called my wife many times using my AT&T calling card. When I got home and received my phone bill several weeks later, I was looking at a charge of $357 just for my use of the calling card. I owed the money. I had used the calling card, and therefore I owed all the money charged me.

But instead of getting upset or beating myself up for running up such a large phone bill, I picked up the phone and called AT&T. I talked to Karen in the Customer Service Department and explained the situation. I asked her if we could do anything to lower those charges. Karen told me that if I signed up for their calling card program, she would retroactively apply the lower rates that the program charged to my December usage. She did tell me there was a monthly charge for this program; it would cost me $1 per month to enroll. I asked her how much doing this would save or cost me.

She calculated the new rates against my December usage and told me that if I signed up for this program, I'd receive a $227 credit against my December bill, and they would charge me just $1 for the last two months. That sounded like a great idea, and I enrolled immediately. Just because I Asked for What I Wanted, even though it wasn't owed to me in the least, I saved $225 off my phone bill. If I hadn't felt worthy of asking, then I would have paid the full amount, and I would have lost out on that wonderful experience.

## Don't expect to receive a positive answer to all your requests, but be grateful when you do.

What has always amazed me is this: how much of what I ask for I really receive. I often just ask for things that I have no expectations of actually receiving; I make the most ridiculous requests at times just to see what will happen. What amazes me on an ongoing basis is how many of these requests are actually fulfilled.

I've walked into stores and seen the perfect items on sale, at prices that I'd gladly pay twice over. But instead of doing so, I'll ask the manager if they'll discount the items even further. About half the time they grant my request, and I pay far less than I would have ever thought possible. Sometimes at dinner at some of the nicer restaurants in my area, I compliment the manager on an excellent meal. I then ask him for complimentary dessert. I tell him if he grants my request I'll tell all my friends about the restaurant. More than half the time, I get a free dessert. Then, of course, I fulfill my part of the bargain and tell my friends about the restaurant. (I'd have told all my friends about it anyway, because it was that good.)

Practice this trait. Just like a professional baseball player takes batting practice, step up to the plate and practice. Ask for What You Want, When You Want It. Don't count the swings and misses, though. See how many of your requests people are willing to fulfill. Don't be upset when they don't do so, and be grateful for those they do fulfill. Search your heart, and when you find you have a deep heartfelt desire, don't hesitate to Ask for What You Want, When You Want It. Be aware of what you are asking for; only ask for that which is your heartfelt desire.

*The Universe will only give you what you ask for.* Spend some time and search your heart. When you ask, be specific in your requests. When negotiating the price of an item, know what you're willing to pay before you begin asking. Then, if you don't get what you want, walk away if you feel the item isn't worth what the other person is asking for it. If you get a better deal than you were willing to accept, be grateful.

Don't gloat. Don't tell the other person, "I was willing to pay twice what you charged me." Neither of these behaviors demonstrates respectful behavior towards the other person or your Self. Accept the gifts the Universe sends to you with respect, generosity, and gratitude. Share your gifts generously and you'll receive many more.

Mike shares his story about learning this lesson:

> In the past, I've been scared to death to ever ask anyone to either do anything for me or to give me something. I couldn't imagine the shame if I asked someone and they turned to me and either laughed at me or told me that I didn't deserve to be given what I asked for. That would be the most humiliating experience I could ever imagine. And I used to be convinced that's exactly what would happen if I asked.

125

*Even when I really wanted someone to help me and I thought they probably would have been glad to do so, I was far too frightened to ask. My family has asked me many times what they could do to help me, and I was always too afraid to tell them for fear they would then reject the request. So, instead, I tried to do everything myself. I was always overwhelmed by the tasks in front of me, and then when I didn't get them all done, I felt terrible because I viewed that as more evidence of how unfit I was as a human being.*

*Then, I learned to Ask for What I Want. I began by asking my closest friends and family for the simplest requests. When they gladly responded with "yes," I then started to ask for a little more. They really seemed happy to finally be able to help me. Several of them even told me they thought I'd been acting like I was too good to accept help, and they were glad to learn that that wasn't the case.*

*For the last couple of months, I've been really working to ask people whenever I have a legitimate need they can help fulfill. Most of the times they respond favorably, although sometimes they tell me "no." I remind myself that, when they say "no," they probably had a great reason for doing so that had nothing to do with me. I also make sure I tell the people how much I appreciate their efforts when they try to help me.*

*Just the other night I went into a fancy restaurant with Christine, my wife. I ordered a large steak and a baked potato. Before the meal came, I had this deep craving for a lobster instead of the steak I ordered. In the past, I'd have said nothing to anyone and just eaten the steak. When I shared how I was feeling with Christine, she reminded me to Ask for What I Want. So I called the waiter over and explained that I'd changed my mind, and then I asked if he could change my order. The waiter said he would check with the cook and let me know what they could do.*

*Now, I'm certain they'd already started to cook the steak. The waiter and the manager came over to the table, and I braced myself to be scolded for trying to change my order. Instead, they said they would gladly change the order, but that doing so would add an additional few minutes before our food was ready. If I'd accept the three-to-five- minute delay, they would gladly change my order. I looked at Christine, and we both said, "Yes, we'll accept that." I know this is a small little step, but I felt wonderful. I Asked for What I Wanted, When I Wanted It— and I got it.*

*I stand amazed at how many of my requests are answered with "yes" these days. It seems people are looking for the opportunity to help one another, and whenever they find that chance they're actually happy to do so. I never have experienced this before. It feels great. I really do see how I'm honoring my Self, how I'm loving my Self by Asking for What I Want, When I Want It.*

When you feel confident in your Self, you Ask for What You Want, When You Want It. To do otherwise is to tell your Self you don't deserve to be loved, that you're not worthy of having your heartfelt desires fulfilled. You're a Child of the Universe, a divine being in your own right. Become as a child. You deserve to have all the greatest gifts this world has to offer. Just feel confident enough to Ask. Ask and you will receive.

## Conclusion: Experiencing your Self with love

We are often sort of mesmerized by the daily tasks of our life, and we can easily become entranced by our routines. It's only when we step back from the trees to view the forest that we can see the three distinct phases of growth that humans transcend on their paths to understanding love. As small children, we are living expressions of love and of our beings, without fears and filters. Then, through our socialization and maturation processes, we learn many fears. As we learn these fears and constraints on our behaviors, we begin our experiences of fear.

These experiences manifest themselves in a lack of Self-love, in every single person on this planet. Out of this belief, we develop many behaviors that demonstrate a lack of respect and love for our Selves. These beliefs and behaviors generate suffering, pain, and frustration in our lives, to varying degrees, all of which demonstrate our lack of Self-love and Self-respect.

When your Self receives those messages enough times, your mind begins to believe in that lack of Self-love as fact. These behaviors become habits that then, in turn, contribute to your generating a life filled with struggle and pain.

But these experiences actually end up serving us by enabling us to experience our Selves as love in later years. These experiences of fear and pain create the contrast that allows us to understand the depth and breadth of love once we transcend these fear-based beliefs. In truth, our experiences of fear create the very foundation for our next step, Enlightenment.

Once we understand that everyone experiences these phases in their lives, we can then give ourselves permission to be human. We can then view these experiences with gratitude, because we see the benefits they provide us in our path to Enlightenment. And once we accept our Selves as worthy human beings, we can begin to experience our Selves with respect and love.

Once we see the patterns in our lives and the resulting patterns in our behaviors, we can begin to change. We can develop new habits that demonstrate love for our Selves. When we treat our Selves with respect and love, we'll then actually experience our Selves as being worthy of love. This experience will build the foundation from which Self-love and Self-respect will sprout.

127

As we Pay Attention to our thoughts and behaviors, we'll notice thoughts and behaviors that don't serve us. We can then choose to change those beliefs and interpretations that cause us to demonstrate a lack of Self-love. We can then also choose to continue those behaviors that serve us to create the lives we most desire. We can choose both of these without judgment. By taking care of our Selves, by learning to live in the moment, and by learning to live in gratitude each minute of the day, we'll begin to build our foundations of Self-love.

As we Take Responsibility for Our Experiences, we'll cease being victims in life and instead claim the power to transform our lives. By Accepting Responsibility, we'll find the lessons in our struggles and claim the power necessary to transform those situations into love and joy. By owning our feelings, by claiming our desires, we'll begin to feel powerful enough to live lives filled with Self-love. Taking Responsibility for living out our lives is an ongoing demonstration of the love of our Selves.

As we Speak Our Truth, we will tell our Selves we deserve to be heard. By being honest and straight with our Selves and others, we will lose the necessity to hide our true Selves from the world. (Speaking Your Truth will cause you to earn back the trust of your friends and family, and even your Self.) As we learn to speak up for our Selves, we can stand boldly in the experience of Self-love.

As we Keep Our Agreements we will demonstrate that we're fulfilling the action part of telling the truth. By Keeping Our Agreements, we'll rebuild trust with our Selves and with others, and begin to understand our Selves as trustworthy and lovable. We will begin to actively demonstrate our Self-love and Self-respect in our actions and behaviors. The Universe will magically align itself in support of our efforts to always Keep Our Agreements. Self-respect and Self-love will follow our commitment in Keeping Our Agreements.

As we Ask for What We Want, When We Want It, we'll claim our right to have our heart's desires fulfilled. We will begin to stake our claims in the Universe to have our divine desires fulfilled and to experience our Selves as prosperous in every aspect of our lives. We will see that gifts and opportunities for abundance and prosperity are our Higher Power's divine gift to each one of us. *No one deserves to be any happier than you do.* It's your divine nature to live a life filled with prosperity. Boldly Ask for What You Want, When You Want It, claim your divine right to happiness, and soon you'll experience genuine Self-love.

As we practice love and respect for our Selves, we'll experience our Selves as deserving only the best the Universe has to offer. As we treat our Selves with love, we'll experience a profound sense of Self-love filling our lives. When we treat our Selves with love and respect, we'll begin to develop a deep, gentle sense of Self-love and Self-respect. By doing so, you'll open your heart and fulfill your divine purpose on this planet: to experience your divinity. As you express the love that's inherent in your heart, you'll feel Spirit in your heart and in your Soul. And that's the experience we all search for, our entire lives.

# Spiritual Truths Discussed in this Chapter

**Asking for What You Want demonstrates to your Self that you deserve to have your heartfelt desires fulfilled.**

When you boldly Ask for What You Want, When You Want It, you're telling your Self you deserve to be heard, you deserve to have your heart's desires fulfilled, you deserve the best the Universe has to offer.

**Spirit desires your life to be filled with prosperity.**

All the great spiritual teachings tell us that our divine nature is to live lives filled with abundance and prosperity. Don't be afraid to live a life filled with Self-love, loving relationships, vitality and health, and material wealth. It's your divine nature to do so.

**Desire is God's way of telling you a gift is already on its way towards you.**

The Universe is a gentle river of energy, carrying the treasures of heaven on its waves. When you open the door to your heart, these gifts will naturally flow into your life. God places desires in your heart to let you know when gifts that will serve you to create the greatest life possible are already flowing your way.

**Don't expect to receive positive answers to all your requests, and be grateful when you do.**

Everyone on this planet has free will. When you make a request, other people have the ability and the right to say "yes" or to say "no" to your request. Don't get upset when they say "no," and be grateful when they say "yes."

Our deepest fear is not that we are inadequate.
Our deepest fear is that we are powerful beyond measure.
It is our Light, not our darkness, that most frightens us.

We ask ourselves, who am I to be brilliant,
gorgeous, talented and fabulous?

You are a child of God.

Your playing small doesn't serve the world! There is a
nothing enlightened about shrinking so that other people
won't feel insecure around you.

We were born to make manifest the glory of God
that is within us.

It's not just in some of us; it's in everyone. And as we
let our own light shine, we unconsciously give other
people permission to do the same.

As we are liberated from our own fear, our presence
automatically liberates others.

— Marianne Williamson

Used by Nelson Mandella in his 1994 Inaugural Speech

# Bibliography

*The Bible According to Einstein* (Jupiter Scientific Publishing Company, New York, NY, 1999).

*Foundations of Unity* (Unity Books, Unity Village, MO).

*The Golden Rule in Ten of the World's Great Religions* (The Foundation for Spiritual Understanding).

*The Sayings of Buddha* (The Ecco Press, Hopewell, NJ, 1991).

*The Torah* (Henry Holt and Company, New York, NY, 1996).

*The Torah: The Five Books of Moses* (The Jewish Publication Society, Jerusalem, 1962).

Jack Ensign Addington, *The Hidden Mystery of the Bible* (Dodd, Mead, and Company, New York, NY, 1969).

Ahmed Ali (trans.), *Al-Qur'an: A Contemporary Translation* (Princeton University Press, Princeton, NJ, 1984).

James Allen, *As a Man Thinketh* (Peter Pauper Press, Inc., White Plains, NY).

Aristotle, *On Man in the Universe* (Gramercy Books, New York, NY, 1943).

Martin Aronson (ed.), *Jesus and Lao Tzu: The Parallel Sayings* (Seastone, Berkeley, CA, 2000).

Richard Bach, *One* (Silver Arrow Books, New York, NY, 1988).

John Bartlett, *Bartlett's Familiar Quotations,* Ninth Edition (Brown, Boston, MA, 1901) (http://www.bartleby.com/99/).

W.W. Bartley, III, *Werner Erhard* (Clarkson N. Potter, New York, NY, 1978).

Father Leo Booth, *The Angel and the Frog: Becoming Your Own Angel* (SCP Limited, Long Beach, CA, 1997).

Father Leo Booth, *The God Game: It's Your Move* (Stillpoint Publishing, Walpole, NH, 1994).

Marcus Borg (ed.), *Jesus and Buddha: The Parallel Sayings* (Ulysses Press, Berkeley, CA, 1997).

John Westerdale Bowker, *World Religions: The Great Faiths Explored & Explained* (Dorling Kindersley Limited, London, UK, 1977).

Denis Brian, *Einstein: A Life* (John Wiley and Sons, Inc., New York, NY, 1996).

Garth Brooks and Hayden Nicholas, *Wherever You Go* (from the *One Emotion* CD) (RCA Records, Nashville, TN, 1994).

Guatama Buddha, Thomas Cleary (trans.), *Dhammapada: The Sayings of Buddha* (Bantam Books, New York, NY, 1995).

Matthew E. Bunson (ed.), *The Wisdom Teachings of the Dalai Lama* (Penguin Books, New York, NY, 1997).

Tolly Burkan and Peggy Dylan Burkan, *Guiding Your Self Into Spiritual Reality* (Reunion Press, Twain Harte, CA, 1983).

Eric Butterworth, *The Concentric Perspective* (Unity Books, Unity Village, MO, 1989).

Eric Butterworth, *Discover the Power Within You* (Harper and Row, San Francisco, CA, 1968).

Eric Butterworth, *In the Flow of Life* (Unity Books, Unity Village, MO, 1982).

H. Emilie Cady, *How I Used Truth* (Unity Books, Unity Village, MO).

H. Emilie Cady, *Lessons in Truth* (Unity Books, Unity Village, MO).

Nigel Calder, *Einstein's Universe* (Crown Publishers, New York, NY, 1979).

Fritjof Capra, *The Tao of Physics* (Shambhala Publications, Inc., Boston, MA, 1975).

Wing-Tsit Chan, *A Sourcebook in Chinese Philosophy* (Princeton University Press, Princeton, NJ, 1963) (http://members.aol.com/pantheism0/changts.htm).

James H. Charlesworth, *Jesus Within Judaism* (Doubleday Dell Publishing Group, Inc., New York, NY, 1988).

Deepak Chopra, *The Seven Spiritual Laws of Success* (Amber-Allen Publishing, San Rafael, CA, 1994).

Thomas Cleary (ed.), *Zen Antics: 100 Stories of Enlightenment* (Shambhala Publications, Inc., Boston, MA, 1993).

Colin Cross, *Who Was Jesus* (Barnes and Noble Books, New York, NY, 1970).

Mihaly Csikszentmihalyi, *The Evolving Self: A Psychology for the Third Millennium* (Harper and Row Publishing, New York, NY, 1993).

Mihaly Csikszentmihalyi, *Flow: The Psychology of Optimal Experience* (Harper and Row Publishing, New York, NY, 1990).

Dalai Lama, His High Holiness, *The Art of Happiness* (Riverhead Books, New York, NY, 1998).

Dalai Lama, His High Holiness, *The Good Heart: A Buddhist Perspective on the Teachings of Jesus* (Wisdom Books, Boston, MA, 1996).

Hugh D'Andrade, *Charles Fillmore: The Life of the Founder of the Unity School of Christianity* (Harper and Row, New York, NY, 1974).

Newton Dillaway (ed.), *The Gospel of Emerson* (Unity Books, Unity Village, MO, 1988).

Wendy Doniger (ed.), *Merriam-Webster's Encyclopedia of World's Religions* (Merriam-Webster, Springfield, MA, 1999).

Mary Baker Eddy, *Unity of God* (The First Church of Christ, Scientist, Boston, MA, 1936).

Albert Einstein, *Albert Einstein: The Cosmic Pantheist* (http://members.aol.com/Heraklitl/einstein.htm, 1999).

Albert Einstein, *Albert Einstein Online* (http://magna.com.au/~prfbrown/albert e.html, 1999).

Albert Einstein, *Ideas and Opinions* (Crown Publishers, New York, NY, 1954).

Albert Einstein, *The Meaning of Relativity* (Princeton University Press, Princeton, NJ, 1922).

Albert Einstein, *The New York Times* (April 25, 1929, p. 60, col. 4).

Albert Einstein, *Out of My Later Years* (Wings Books, New York, NY, 1956).

Albert Einstein, Boris Podolsky, and Nathan Rosen, *Can the Quantum Mechanical Description of Physical Reality Be Considered Complete?* (*Physical Review*, 1937, Vol. 47, p. 777).

Mark Epstein, M.D., *Going to Pieces Without Falling Apart: A Buddhist Perspective on Wholeness* (Broadway Books, New York, NY, 1998).

Kathleen Fackelmann, *The Power of Prayer (USA Today,* July 18, 2000, p. 7D).

James Fadiman and Robert Frager (eds.), *The Essential Sufism* (Harper Collins, San Francisco, CA, 1997).

Carl Frederick, *EST: Playing the Game the New Way* (Delacorte Press, New York, NY, 1974).

Charles Fillmore, *Atom-Smashing Power of Mind* (Unity Books, Unity Village, MO, 1949).

Charles Fillmore, *Prosperity* (Unity Books, Unity Village, MO).

Charles Fillmore, *The Revealing Word* (Unity Books, Unity Village, MO).

Charles Fillmore, *Talks on Truth* (Unity Books, Unity Village, MO).

Albrecht Flossing, *Albert Einstein* (Penguin Books, New York, NY, 1997).

Emmet Fox, *The Sermon on the Mount* (Harper and Row Publishers, New York, NY, 1934).

Emmet Fox, *The Ten Commandments* (Harper and Row Publishers, New York, NY, 1943).

Kahlil Gibran, *Jesus the Son of Man* (Alfred A. Knopf, Inc., New York, NY, 1928).

Kahlil Gibran, *The Prophet* (Alfred A. Knopf, Inc., New York, NY, 1952).

Douglas Gillette, M.A., M. Div., *The Shaman's Secret: The Lost Resurrection Teachings of the Ancient Maya* (Bantam Books, New York, NY, 1997).

Joseph F. Girzone, *Joshua, a Parable for Today* (Richelieu Court Publishers, Kendall Park, NY, 1983).

Joseph F. Girzone, *A Portrait of Jesus* (Doubleday, New York, NY, 1998).

Joel S. Goldsmith, *Consciousness in Transition: Metaphysical Notes* (Acropolis Books, Lakewood, CO, 1997).

Robert M. Grant and David Noel Freedman, *The Secret Sayings of Jesus* (Barnes and Nobles Books, New York, NY, 1960).

Susan Hayward, *A Book of Insight: Guide for the Advanced Soul* (Little, Brown, and Company, Boston, MA, 1984).

Lewis C. Henry (ed.), *Five Thousand Quotations for All Occasions* (Doubleday and Company, Garden City, NY, 1945).

Benjamin Hoff, *The Tao of Pooh* (Penguin Books USA, Inc., New York, NY, 1982).

Ernest Holmes, *How to Use The Science of Mind* (Dodd, Mead, and Company, New York, NY, 1950).

Ernest Holmes, *The Science of Mind* (G.P. Putnam's Sons, New York, NY, 1938).

Mary-Alice Jafolla, *Simple Truth: A Basic Guide to Metaphysics* (Unity Books, Unity Village, MO, 1982).

John-Roger, *Spiritual Warrior* (Mandeville Press, CA, 1998).

Ken Keyes, Jr., and Bruce (Tolly) Burkan, *How to Make Your Life Work; or, Why Aren't You Happy?* (Living Love Publications, St. Mary, KY, 1974).

Charles Layman (ed.), *The Interpreter's One-Volume Commentary on the Bible* (Abindgton Press, TN, 1971).

Lama Surya Das, *Awakening the Buddha Within: Tibetan Wisdom for the Western World* (Broadway Books, New York, NY, 1997).

Lao-Tzu, Thomas Cleary (trans.), *The Essential Tao* (HarperSanFrancisco, San Francisco, CA, 1991).

Lao-Tzu, Man-Ho Kwok, Martin Palmer, and Jay Ramsey (trans.), *The Illustrated Tao Te Ching* (Barnes and Noble Books, Inc., New York, NY, 1993).

Lao-Tzu, Stephen Mitchell (trans.), *Tao Te Ching: A New English Version* (Harper and Row Publishers, New York, NY, 1988).

James C. Lewis, *The Key to Spiritual Growth* (Unity Books, Unity Village, MO, 1985).

John R. Mabry, M.A., *God as Nature Sees God: A Christian Reading of the Tao Te Ching* (Element, Rockport, MA, 1994).

Michael A. Maday (ed.), *New Thought For a New Millennium: Twelve Powers for the 21st Century* (Unity Books, Unity Village, MO, 1998).

Daniel C. Matt, Ph.D., *God & the Big Bang: Discovering Harmony Between Science & Spirituality* (Jewish Lights Publishing, Woodstock, VT, 1996).

Wayne A. Meeks, *The Origins of Christian Morality* (Yale University Press, New Haven, CT, 1993).

Marvin W. Meyer (trans.), *The Secret Teachings of Jesus: Four Gnostic Gospels* (Random House Publishing, Inc., New York, NY, 1984).

Mary Manin Morrissey, *Building Your Field of Dreams* (Bantam Books, New York, NY, 1996).

Mary Manin Morrissey, Director and Senior Minister at the Living Enrichment Center, various sermons in the *Life Key Series* (The Living Enrichment Center, Wilsonville, OR).

Toshihiko Maruta, M.D., Robert C. Colligan, Ph.D., Michael Malinchoc, M.D., and Kenneth P. Offord, *Optimists vs. Pessimists: Survival Rates Among Medical Patients Over A 30-Year Period* (*Mayo Foundation for Medical Education and Research*, Vol. 75, Number 2, February 2000).

Barabara Stoler Miller (trans.), *The Bhagavbad-Gita: Krishna's Course in Time of War* (Columbia University Press, New York, NY, 1986).

A. A. Milne, *The House at Pooh Corner* (Dutton's Children's Books, New York, NY, 1956).

Jeffrey Moses, *Oneness: Great Principles Shared by All Religions* (Fawcett Columbine, New York, NY, 1989).

Joseph Murphy, *The Amazing Laws of Cosmic Mind Power* (Prentice Hall, Paramus, NJ, 1965).

Caroline Myss, Ph.D., *Anatomy of the Spirit* (Harmony Books, New York, NY, 1996).

Neville, *The Law and the Promise* (DeVorss and Company, Marina Del Ray, CA, 1961).

Dean Ornish, M.D., *Love & Survival: The Scientific Basis for the Healing Power of Intimacy* (HarperCollins Publishing, New York, NY, 1998).

Abraham Pais, *'Subtle is the Lord': The Science and the Life of Albert Einstein* (Oxford University Press, Oxford, UK, 1982).

Barry Parker, *Einstein's Dream: The Search for a Unified Theory of the Universe* (Plenum Press, New York, NY, 1986).

Candace B. Pert, Ph.D., *Molecules of Emotion: Why You Feel the Way You Feel* (Scribner, New York, NY, 1997).

Steven Pinker, *How the Mind Works* (W.W. Norton and Company, New York, NY, 1997).

Steven Pinker, *The Language Instinct: How the Mind Creates* (HarperPerennial, New York, NY, 1994).

James Redfield, *The Celestine Prophecy* (Warner Books, Inc., New York, NY, 1993).

Melinda Ribner, *Everyday Kabbalah: A Practical Guide to Jewish Meditation, Healing, and Personal Growth* (Carol Publishing Group, Toronto, Ontario, Canada, 1998).

David Rosen, M.D., *The Tao of Jung* (Penguin Books, New York, NY, 1996).

Don Miguel Ruiz, *The Four Agreements: A Toltec Wisdom Book* (Amber-Allen Publishing, San Rafeal, CA, 1997).

Gerald L. Schroeder, *The Science of God: The Convergence of Scientific and Biblical Wisdom* (The Free Press, New York, NY, 1997).

Helen Schucman and William Thetford, *A Course of Miracles* (Foundation for Inner Peace, Tiburon, CA, 1975).

Jane Self, Ph.D., *60 Minutes and the Assassination of Werner Erhard: A True Story* (Breakthru Publishing, Houston, TX, 1992).

Thomas J. Shahan, S.T.D., J.U.L., *The Beginnings of Christianity* (Benzinger Brothers, New York, NY, 1903).

Imelda Octavia Shanklin, *What Are You?* (Unity Press, Unity Village, MO, 1995).

Arvind Sharma (ed.), *Our Religions* (HarperSanFrancisco, San Francisco, CA, 1995).

Thomas Shepherd, *Friends in High Places* (Unity Books, Unity Village, MO, 1985).

Huston Smith, *The World's Religions* ((HarperSanFrancisco, San Francisco, CA, 1991).

Ron Smothermon, M.D., *Winning Through Enlightenment* (Context Publishing, CA, 1997).

Naomi Stephan, Ph.D., *Fulfill Your Soul's Purpose: Ten Creative Paths to Your Life* (Stillpoint Publishing, Walpole, NH, 1994).

Nathan Stone, *Names of God* (Moody Press, Chicago, IL, 1944).

Swami Prabhavananda, *The Sermon on the Mount According to Vendata* (Vendata Press, Hollywood, CA, 1913).

William Irwin Thompson, *Coming into Being* (St. Martin's Press, New York, NY, 1996).

Frank J. Tipler, *The Physics of Immortality: Modern Cosmology, God and the Resurrection of the Dead* (Doubleday Publishing, New York, NY, 1994).

Gerald Tomlinson, *Treasury of Religious Quotations* (Prentice-Hall, Englewood Cliffs, NJ, 1991).

Thomas Troward, *Bible Mystery and Bible Meaning* (Dodd, Mead, and Company, New York, NY, 1913).

Thomas Troward, *The Creative Process in the Individual* (G.P. Putnam's Sons, New York, NY, 1915).

Geza Vermes, *The Complete Dead Sea Scrolls in English* (The Penguin Press, New York, NY, 1997).

Neale Donald Walsch, *Conversations with God: an uncommon dialogue, Book 1* (Hampton Roads Publishing Company, Inc., 1995).

Neale Donald Walsch, *Conversations with God: an uncommon dialogue, Book 2* (Hampton Roads Publishing Company, Inc., 1997).

Liao Waysun, *The Essence of T'ai Chi* (Shambhala Publications, Inc.) (http://www.geocities.com/Tokyo/Harbor/2125/TaiChi.html).

White Eagle, *Jesus, Teacher and Healer* (University Printing House, Oxford, UK, 1985).

Marianne Williamson, *A Return to Love* (HarperCollins Publishers, Inc., New York, NY, 1992).

A.N. Wilson, *Jesus: A Life* (W.W. Norton and Company, New York, NY, 1992).

Ian Wilson, *Jesus: The Evidence: The Latest Research and Discoveries Investigated* (HarperCollins, San Francisco, CA, 1996).

Fred Alan Wolf, Ph.D., *The Eagle's Quest: A Physicist Finds Scientific Truth at the Heart of the Shamanic World* (Simon and Schuster, New York, NY, 1991).

# Endnotes

Introduction

[1] Carl Jung, quoted in *New Thought for a New Millennium*, p. 127.

Part One: A New Perspective

[1] Ywahoo Dhyani, *Voices of Our Ancestors: Cherokee Teachings from the Wisdom Fire* (Shambhala Publications, Inc., Boston, MA, 1987) as quoted in *The God Game: It's Your Move*, p. 27.

Chapter One: You Are Not Alone

[1] White Eagle, *Jesus, Teacher and Healer*, p. 98.

[2] Fred Alan Wolf, Ph.D., *The Eagle's Quest: A Physicist Finds Scientific Truth at the Heart of the Shamanic World*, p. 120.

[3] James Allen, *As a Man Thinketh*, p. 15.

[4] Ron Smothermon, M.D., *Winning Through Enlightenment*, p. 2.

[5] Sufi Sheikh Kashani, *The Essential Sufism*, p. 67.

[6] Bernie Siegel, M.D., *New Thought for a New Millennium*, p. 123.

Chapter Two: The Path to Enlightenment

[1] Mihaly Csikszentmihalyi, Ph.D., *Flow: The Psychology of Optimal Experience*, p. 9.

[2] Daniel C. Matt, Ph.D., *God & the Big Bang: Discovering Harmony Between Science & Spirituality*, p. 28.

[3] Albrecht Flossing, *Albert Einstein*, p. 736.

[4] James Dillet Freemeent, *New Thought for a New Millennium*, p. 97.

[5] Stretton Smith, *Stretton Smith's 4T Prosperity Program*, p. 77.

[6] Daniel C. Matt, Ph.D., *God & the Big Bang: Discovering Harmony Between Science & Spirituality*, p. 63.

[7] Jim Rosemergy, *New Thought for a New Millennium*, p. 23.

[8] Swami Prabhavananda, *The Sermon on the Mount According to the Vedanta*, p. 44.

[9] *The Torah: The Five Books of Moses*, p. 4.

[10] Eric Butterworth, *The Concentric Perspective: What's In It for Me?*, p. 8.

[11] Marvin W. Meyer (trans.), *The Secret Teachings of Jesus: Four Gnostic Gospels*, p. 41.

[12] Swami Prabhavananda, *The Sermon on the Mount According to the Vedanta*, pp. 45-46.

[13] Stretton Smith, *Stretton Smith's 4T Prosperity Program*, p. 124.

[14] Dean Ornish, M.D., *Love & Survival: The Scientific Basis for the Healing Power of Intimacy*, back cover.

[15] James Allen, *As a Man Thinketh*, pp. 32-33.

[16] Candace B. Pert, Ph.D., *Molecules of Emotion: Why You Feel the Way You Feel*, p. 208.

[17] Carolyn Stearns, *Molecules of Emotion: Why You Feel the Way You Feel*, p. 244.

[18] Lao-Tzu, Stephen Mitchell (trans.), *Tao Te Ching*, Chapter 2.

[19] Gregory Bateson, *Molecules of Emotion: Why You Feel the Way You Feel*, p. 257.

[20] Lao-Tzu, Stephen Mitchell (trans.), *Tao Te Ching*, Chapter 5.

[21] Swami Prabhavananda, *The Sermon on the Mount According to Vedanta*, p. 35.

[22] Gerald L. Schroeder, Ph.D., *The Science of God: The Convergence of Scientific and Biblical Wisdom*, p. 17.

[23] Lao-Tzu, as quoted in *The Tao of Physics*, p. 106.

[24] James Fadiman and Roger Frager (eds.), *The Essential Sufism*, p. 52.

[25] Gerald L. Schroeder, Ph.D., *The Science of God: The Convergence of Scientific and Biblical Wisdom*, p. 11.

[26] Some of the stories that use the term "forty" as a metaphor for "until completion" are:

- It rained for forty days and forty nights (*Book of Genesis* 7:4).
- The flood lasted forty days (*Book of Genesis* 7:17).
- Isaac was forty years old when he took Rebekah as his wife (*Book of Genesis* 25:20).
- Esau was forty years old when he took Judith to be his wife (*Book of Genesis* 26:34).
- Egypt mourned for forty days for Jacob, Joseph's father (*Book of Genesis* 50:3).
- The Israelites ate manna for forty years (*Book of Exodus* 16:35).
- Moses sent members of each of the twelve tribes to search for the Promised Land; they returned from their search after forty days (*Book of Numbers* 13:25).
- God sent the Israelites to wander in the desert for forty years (*Book of Numbers* 32:13).
- Moses was on the mount for forty days before receiving the Ten Commandments (*Book of Exodus* 24:18).
- Jesus fasted for forty days and forty nights when he was tempted by the devil (*Gospel of Matthew* 4:2).
- Jesus visits the disciples for forty days after his resurrection (*Book of Acts* 1:3).
- Moses was forty years old when he went to Egypt to free the slaves (*Book of Acts* 7:23).

[27] Paul Carus (comp.), *The Teachings of Buddha*, p. 23.

[28] Paul Carus (comp.), *The Teachings of Buddha*, p. 23.

[29] James Fadiman and Roger Frager (eds.), *The Essential Sufism*, p. 73.

[30] Kahlil Gibran, *The Prophet*, pp. 29-30.

[31] James Allen, *As a Man Thinketh*, p. 17.

[32] Ron Smothermon, M.D., *Winning Through Enlightenment*, p. 51.

[33] Bernie Siegel, M.D., *New Thought for a New Millennium*, p. 126.

[34] Ralph Waldo Emerson, *The Gospel of Emerson*, p. 96.

[35] Sufi Sheikh Abdul Qadir al-Jalami, *The Essential Sufism*, pp. 103–104.

Chapter Three: Pay Attention

[1] Carlos Castaneda, *The Teachings of Don Juan*, as quoted in *The Tao of Physics*, p. 16.

[2] Eric Butterworth, *In the Flow of Life*, p. 70.

[3] Thomas Cleary, *Dhammapada: The Sayings of Buddha*, p. 18.

[4] Gautama Buddha, Thomas Cleary (trans.), *Dhammapada: The Sayings of Buddha*, p. 44.

[5] Stretton Smith, *Stretton Smith's 4T Prosperity Program*, p. 32.

[6] Jane Self, Ph.D., *60 Minutes and the Assassination of Werner Erhard: A True Story*, p. 16.

[7] Sufi Sheikh Tosun Bayrak, *The Essential Sufism*, p. 71.

[8] Mihaly Csikszentmihalyi, Ph.D., *Flow: The Psychology of Optimal Experience*, p. 31.

[9] Ron Smothernmon, M.D., *Winning Through Enlightenment*, p. 77.

[10] Carl Frederick, *EST: Playing the Game the New Way*, p. 27.

[11] Tolly Burkan and Peggy Dylan Burkan, *Guiding Yourself Into a Spiritual Reality*, p. 13.

[12] Eric Butterworth, *The Concentric Perspective: What's In It for Me?*, p. 17.

[13] Candace B. Pert, Ph.D., *Molecules of Emotion: Why You Feel the Way You Feel*, p. 265.

[14] Charles Fillmore, as quoted in *Stretton Smith's 4T Prosperity Program*, p. 10.

[15] Eric Butterworth, *The Concentric Perspective: What's In It for Me?*, p. 33.

[16] Stretton Smith, *Stretton Smith's 4T Prosperity Program*, p. 53.

Chapter Four: Take Responsibility for Your Experience

[1] Lao-Tzu, Stephen Mitchell (trans.), *Tao Te Ching*, Chapter 79.

[2] Jesus as quoted by Richard Patton, *The Autobiography of Jesus of Nazareth and the Missing Years*, p. 208.

[3] Ron Smothermon, M.D., *Winning Through Enlightenment*, p. 48.

[4] James Allen, *As a Man Thinketh*, p. 9.

[5] Ron Smothermon, M.D., *Winning Through Enlightenment*, p. 15.

[6] Father Leo Booth, *The Angel and the Frog: Becoming Your Own Angel*, p. 133.

[7] Ron Smothermon, M.D., *Winning Through Enlightenment*, p. 76.

[8] Candace B. Pert, Ph.D., *Molecules of Emotion: Why You Feel the Way You Feel*, p. 193.

[9] Barbara Marx Hubbard, as quoted in *New Thought for a New Millennium*, p. 176.

[10] Lao-Tzu, Stephen Mitchell (trans.), *Tao Te Ching*, Chapter 62.

Chapter Five: Speak Your Truth

[1] Stretton Smith, *Stretton Smith's 4T Prosperity Program*, p. 106.

[2] Ralph Waldo Emerson, *The Gospel of Emerson*, p. 22.

[3] Father Leo Booth, *The God Game: It's Your Move*, p. 25.

[4] Marvin W. Meyer (trans.), *The Secret Teachings of Jesus: Four Gnostic Gospels*, p. 9.

Chapter Six: Keep Your Agreements

[1] White Eagle, *Jesus, Teacher and Healer*, p. 43.

[2] Ron Smothermon, M.D., *Winning Through Enlightenment*, p. 74.

[3] Charles Fillmore, *Talks on Truth*, p. 9.

Chapter Seven: Ask for What You Want

[1] Lao-Tzu, Stephen Mitchell (trans.), *Tao Te Ching*, Chapter 5.

[2] Bernie Siegel, M.D., *New Thought for a New Millennium*, pp. 128-129.

[3] Mihaly Csikszentmihalyi, Ph.D., *Flow: The Psychology of Optimal Experience*, p. 45.

[4] Bernie Siegel, M.D., *New Thought for a New Millennium*, p. 126.

[5] Lao-Tzu, Stephen Mitchell (trans.), *Tao Te Ching*, Chapter 8.

[6] Lao-Tzu, Stephen Mitchell (trans.), *Tao Te Ching*, Chapter 5.

[7] H. Emilie Cady, as quoted in *Foundations of Unity*, p. 20.

# Acknowledgments

I can never express the importance of the support, love, and undying patience my late wife Cheryl demonstrated. She endured listening to more workshops and read and helped edit more versions of this book than either one of us care to think about. Cheryl, you are my tower of strength. Even while you were faced with your own life challenges, you still provided unlimited love and support for my passions. Your unlimited courage inspires me today and will always continue to do so. Your love, which is eternal, is a rock I lean on when I get tired or discouraged. You are my hero. I admire you, I respect you, and I love you. Thank you for being you and sharing your life with me. You honored me with your love and your presence in my life. I can never express the depth and breadth of my love for you, a love that will last until the end of time. In a million years I would never be able to share how much of a contribution you made in my life, even over such a short period of time. I understand you just did not have any more you needed to learn in this life, and I am grateful you chose to share yourself with me. When I feel the gentle breeze brushing past my face, I will also know it is the wind wafting downward off the wings of the angel I shared my life with. I love you Cheryl, now, always, forever.

I would also like to express my gratitude to Tolly Burkan for generously allowing me the use of his Five Points of Power. The first time I was exposed to these ideas, I immediately saw their application for Self-love. Tolly has graciously given me permission to include them in my teachings. For this, I'm grateful. Thank you, Tolly.

I wish to thank my two beautiful golden retrievers, Queen Maya and Joshua. You two kept me company during those late nights writing in the library. You kept my feet warm by sleeping on them and letting me know you were there. Because your ability to both read these words and feel appreciation for this gesture may be limited, I shall have to find a different way to say "Thank you." I have some specials treat for you: a fresh bone from the butcher shop and a long belly rub and an old-fashioned ear scratch each.

Also, I would like to acknowledge and express my gratitude to those people who have contributed to this material. Anton Marco (www.mentorwordwright.com) coached me and provided me with editing services. Jennifer Hynes, Ph.D. (of Lohman Letters) provided additional editing and proofreading services. Kathy Paparchontis (of K & D, Associates) did the indexing. Mary Clark Karriker (of Creative Sky Communications) provided the production layout and cover design. I thank each one of you for your contribution to transforming this material into a book.

And, finally, I thank you, my reader, for allowing me to share with you my gift, from my soul to yours. I pray that this book helps you to accelerate your own journey from "less-than" to experiencing your very own life filled with joy and happiness.

# INDEX

# INDEX OF PASSAGES

# Quantum Spirituality

## Visit Online

Please visit us at www.quantum-spirituality.com or www.self-love.com for more information, Grant's public appearances, or the schedule for future workshops and retreats.

▲ **Unlimited Abundance & Prosperity**

▲ **Five Secrets to Self-Love**

▲ **Quantum Power of Faith**

▲ **Experiencing Divinity in Relationships**

## Exciting life-changing retreats!

Grant has been actively involved in the arena of metaphysical studies for the last decade. Grant emerges as a compassionate leader with special insights from his extensive research and years as a student under some of the great teachers of our time. Grant has been leading and facilitating workshops, seminars, and study groups for the last eight years and brings to light **tools you will want and need** for your unique spiritual journey.

## Coming Soon

Watch for **Quantum Power of Thought** due in late 2003.

## Bookstores

**5 Secrets to Self-Love** and **Quantum Spirituality** are available online or through book retailers.

www.amazon.com

www.bn.com

Quantum Spirituality Press ▪ P.O. Box 529 ▪ Chester, New Jersey 07930-0088